Cookie Crumbs

AN AUTOBI**DOG**RAPHY

KEN SMITH

ISBN 978-1-950818-69-3 (paperback)

Copyright © 2020 by Ken Smith

All rights reserved. No part of this publication may be reproduced, distributed, or transmitted in any form or by any means, including photocopying, recording, or other electronic or mechanical methods without the prior written permission of the publisher. For permission requests, solicit the publisher via the address below.

Rushmore Press LLC
1 888 733 9607
www.rushmorepress.com

Printed in the United States of America

This book is dedicated to my wife and Cookie's mom, Laurie. For so long we were a pack of three: Mom, Dad, and Cookie, each supporting and protecting the other.

Cookie loved her mom as deeply as she loved life itself. They shared the same heart, and they are soul hearts forever.

It was Laurie who communicated best with Cookie. It was she who made Cookie's adventures in the great indoors more meaningful and memorable.

Laurie has been very patient and understanding during the writing of this book. She allowed me the time and space needed to reflect, collect my thoughts, and enable my words to flow freely and passionately.

In addition, she offered valuable input and insight into the writing of many of Cookie's adventures, providing a feminine perspective. More than once, her recollection of a particular adventure differed slightly from my own. She often recalled a different detail or reaction. This only served to allow that story to come to life more fully.

I am so grateful that Cookie had such an awesome mom and that I have such a supportive wife.

Writing *Cookie Crumbs* has truly been a pack effort.

Introduction

Perhaps the greatest story ever written is the story of man and his best friend, the dog. Its pages abound with tales of adventure, courage and loyalty – pages that continue to be written every day by both man and dog.

Cookie Crumbs is the story of my dog. Each page is like a little crumb of Cookie's life left behind for us to remember and enjoy.

Most pages are filled with recipes for canine fun and are sure to leave you smiling or laughing. Some may fill you with wonder, and a few may even break your heart.

In many ways, Cookie lived the life of ten dogs. Her life was spent adventuring into the great outdoors as well as the great indoors. As you flip the pages of *Cookie Crumbs* and discover the many tales of her amazing life, Cookie will reel you in hook, line, and sinker.

Above all else, Cookie was fiercely loyal to her pack and swimming was her life's passion.

Cookie was keenly aware and very concerned about the safety and welfare of all creatures. She especially sensed the distress and discomfort of dogs that entered the animal control shelter where I worked and where she lived. I could tell she looked to me to provide help and relief to them.

In her thirteenth year, Cookie set off on her adventure into the great unknown. It was all too soon for us, and we miss her terribly.

This book is a celebration of our dog and her life. We are fortunate to be able to share her story with you.

It is our hope that *Cookie Crumbs* will inspire you to add your own special pages to that great and timeless story of man and his best friend, the dog.

May it also move you to take action in the defense of so many of our neglected and abused furry friends.

Finally, it is our hope that reading *Cookie Crumbs* will awaken or renew within you a faith that best friends are forever.

Special Note to Readers

Cookie was extremely expressive and communicative; translating this book from Labrador to English was very easy.

Stories were compiled as they occurred throughout Cookie's thirteen-year life

In this way, this book can be considered to be an autobi**dog**raphy.

PART ONE

The Promise

I was just eight weeks old when I became Dad's dog.

As we rode along in the ol' black truck on our way home that very day, I lay in Dad's lap. While he was petting me, he told me that I was a Labrador retriever, a breed of sporting dog. He said that a dog like me needs lots of outdoor activity, especially swimming, to be happy and to become the dog I was made to be.

He promised me that he would take me on outdoor adventures every day and give me the freedom to explore my world untethered. He also promised me that he would take me swimming and retrieving just as often as the weather allowed.

I trusted my dad and believed every word of what he promised me.

A Fortune Cookie

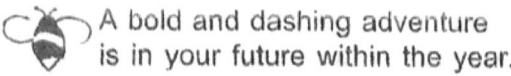 A bold and dashing adventure is in your future within the year.

Fortune cookie slip

Shortly after Christmas, Dad was out for a meal and was served a fortune cookie that read "A bold and dashing adventure is in your future within the year."

For some reason, Dad decided to save the message in his fortune cookie.

About a week later, he got a call from his friend Greg. He knew that Dad was thinking about getting a dog. He told Dad of a young couple who was giving away, free to a good home, an eight-week-old Labrador retriever puppy.

I was running around in the front yard when Dad drove up. He picked me up and promised that he would give me a good home and take really good care of me. So just like that, I rode home in the ol' black truck, laying in Dad's lap.

After we got home, Dad remembered his fortune cookie and said he was sure that I was going to be his bold and dashing adventure. To honor his good fortune, Dad told me that my name should be Cookie.

That is how I came to be Dad's dog and how I got my name.

Clumsy

So began my life of adventure and fun.
    I tripped and stumbled over everything: toys, sticks, rocks, holes, and curbs. I was clumsy and not very well coordinated.

The world was so big and formidable.

But day by day, I grew and developed and learned.

Dad kept me busy and worked me hard. I slept when I wasn't out exploring the world.

Every day was challenging, and I loved it. All my senses were being awakened and stimulated: sight, sound, scent, taste, and touch. I was alive, and it was amazing.

Nog Dog

Puppy dog Cookie

I was the runt of my litter, so Dad has given me eggs beat in milk since I was a baby. He says it makes my coat shine and builds strong bones.

When I first came home to Dad, I got two or three eggnogs a week. Now that I am grown, I still get them but not as many.

Everyone says I have a coat that glistens, and Dad says it is because of the eggnogs and the fact that I swim every day in a pond filled with snow melt and spring water.

My vet also says I have a lot of bone mass and that part of the reason I do is because of the eggnogs.

Dad likes to spice things up for me, so when he makes me my eggnogs, sometimes he puts in just a little nutmeg or vanilla.

I call the nutmeg ones Nut Nogs and the vanilla ones 'Nilla Nogs.

The Clothes Hamper

After Dad brought me home as a puppy, it didn't take long for me to imprint on him and bond with him.

He was the first two-legged I had ever been around on a daily basis. I got to know him by the sound of his voice, the feel of his touch, and his scent.

It was easy being around Dad. I felt very safe and protected. He was very kind to me; he gave me lots of attention and affection.

Next to the bed, there was a small basket filled with Dad's dirty clothes. They had Dad's scent. It was natural for me to climb into that clothes hamper whenever I was tired and ready for a nap or when it was time for bed.

I would burrow down into his dirty clothes and bury myself in his scent. Snuggling into Dad's clothes made me feel safe and secure. I was totally protected and close to Dad. I had no cares in the world and slept soundly.

It was heavenly.

Dog Piling

When I was a baby dog with my canine mother and the rest of us pups, we crawled all over each other and slept together in a big warm ball. The two-leggeds call this dog piling; we four-leggeds just call it safeguarding the pack.

Dad has always allowed me to do what comes natural to a dog like me. He lets me dog pile all over him. I crawl onto him and sometimes lay on top of him when he is reclining in his La Z Boy.

At night, I sleep on top of Dad at the foot of the bed. It is very cozy; after all, we are just a pack of dogs that are safe and snug as bugs.

Squeaker Time

Dad says he wants me to be a puppy for a long time, so he still plays with me every day. He never discourages me and always takes time to play with me whenever I want.

I have several favorite toys. One is a pull sock that Dad made by tying two old socks together with a big knot in the middle. Sometimes I throw it around, and sometimes I have a good tug of war with Dad.

My Smurf and my Dino are my squeaker toys. I love to shake them and make them squeak. It is just like catching a mouse and is good practice in case I have to catch my own dinner.

When I wear out my squeakers, I pull all of the stuffing out of them and also pull the squeaker itself out. Then Dad knows it is time to replace them; he usually has a new Smurf and Dino on hand just in case one needs replacing.

I love playing with my toys and want to be a puppy forever.

Blanky

I miss Dad during the day when he is at work or away at a meeting. So to keep him close to me, I sometimes take one of his T-shirts or a pair of his socks or underwear and drag them onto the bed with me. That way, Dad is close by, and I am able to keep his scent with me.

Sometimes even when Dad is home, I like to lay on his stuff, and I am always dragging his clothes out and scattering them all over the house or the yard.

Dad never gets after me for this; he says it is just natural for me as a retriever to do this sort of thing. He doesn't want to discourage me from feeling close to him. I got a good dad.

Playing Catch

Dad and I play catch with my green tennis ball. Dad rolls it to me, and I grab it with my mouth and then toss it back to him. We throw it back and forth to each other like this a half-a-dozen times or more.

Then Dad throws my tennis ball up in the air. I jump up high and catch it in my mouth.

Dad says I am a natural centerfielder. I love to play catch, so "Put me in Dad; I'm ready to play."

Water Daughter

Dad says I was swimming before I was walking. An exaggeration for sure, but having been born on Thanksgiving Day, spring came quickly.

It was March. I was just four months old, and the snow and ice on the beaver pond had melted.

Dad would wade out into the pond with me in his arms. Then he would just put me in the water. I was clumsy and splashed the water with my paws, but I made it back to shore. Every day, we did five or six laps like this. It didn't take long before I wasn't splashing the water; Dad said I was moving through the water quickly and quietly, just like a canoe.

Then one day, Dad just waded out into the water without me. And just like that, I followed him into the water and was swimming before I was five months old. My first year, I went swimming two hundred days, and I have been swimming ever since.

Dad says that I love swimming so much and have so much fun that he calls me his water daughter.

Water Dog

Swimming flipped a switch in me that turned me into a soaking wet, waterlogged water dog.

It was the call of the wild.

Soon, I was swimming in the river, in the lake, and in the beaver pond.

By the time fall came, I was swimming in the morning, in the evening, and even in my dreams all night long.

With Dad's help and encouragement, I answered my call of the wild.

Disc Dog

Soon after I became a strong swimmer, Dad began to teach me to retrieve objects he threw into the water.

He tossed brightly colored round discs, called frisbees, into the lake. They caught my attention, and retrieving them came natural for me. Time after time, I would retrieve the disc and swim back to Dad with it in my mouth. I would drop it pretty close by Dad so he could throw it out into the lake again.

Sometimes, the discs got flipped over in the water and would start to slowly sink. I had to put my head underwater to grab them quickly before they could sink to the bottom of the lake.

I wore Dad's arm out retrieving those frisbees. He would laugh and call me his water-dancing disc dog.

Bobbing for Apples

Fall is the best time of year in the mountains. There are still some wildflowers left. It is cooler; Dad and I are still swimming every day in the beaver pond. Best of all, trees turn color! Yellow, gold, brown, orange, and even red are everywhere. Dad says it is almost as spectacular as New England in the fall.

Also in the fall, apples are ripe for eating. Up past the beaver pond, there is an apple orchard. It was part of an old dairy homestead. Every day, Dad and I pass the orchard on our way up to Cottonwood Grove.

On the way back, Dad picks two or three big apples, and we bring them to the beaver pond. Dad throws one in, and I swim out to retrieve it.

They are hard to grab in the water. Every time I grab for one, it goes underwater and gets away from me; then it pops up somewhere else. Finally, I have to put my head underwater, and then I can usually get hold of the apple. On the way back to shore, I chew the apple up into pieces so Dad has to throw one of the other ones in for me.

He gets a big kick out of all this and says that in the fall, Cookie bobs for apples.

Draft Beer

Dad likes draft beer and draft root beer. He says I will never be old enough to drink beer and that root beer isn't good for me.

So what I really like is draft water. Yes, that's right. In spring and summer, when I want a cold one, I don't mess around with drinking out of my water bowl. No, not me; I'll take mine right out of the tap.

Dad just turns on the outside faucet and I guzzle down some good old black dog water.

The Upper Paw

My pack is small; it's just me and my dad. Dad doesn't realize it, but I am the leader of our pack: the Alpha female.

At night when it's time for bed, I usually get my spot at the foot of the bed. When Dad gets into bed, I give him a good tussle and make him earn his place in bed. It's a tough world for us four-leggeds, and I need to toughen up Dad 'cause he's at a disadvantage, having only two legs.

Another thing that the leader of the pack must do is to have her paw on top always. This shows pack dominance. If it happens that Dad does have a hand, arm, or leg over me, I always pull my paw out from under and put it on top. I must have the upper paw.

The Duck Pond

The duck pond is different from the beaver pond where I swim. The duck pond is actually inside the house.

It all started because I am a retriever and need to retrieve something, anything.

During the day and even at night, I love to play. So from time to time, I retrieve dirty socks from the laundry hamper and drag them all over the house and even outside.

This soon became quite a game for me and Dad. I would retrieve socks, shirts, and even Dad's underwear from the hamper. Then the chase was on.

I never tore or chewed anything up; I just love to retrieve.

Finally, Dad began calling the laundry hamper the duck pond, and the dirty clothes in the hamper became known as dead ducks. Sometimes, the house and the yard are strewn with the dead ducks that I have retrieved.

The Wind

A hard wind has always scared me.

Dad says it is probably because when I was a baby, I belonged to a young couple who worked all day and left me in the garage all by myself.

He says there must have been a hard wind that made a lot of noise and maybe knocked a few things down.

I probably got scared and had no one to protect me, so I found a place to hide until the wind was gone

Since then, every time there is a bad wind, I get scared.

At least now when the wind does blow hard, Dad lets me come in the house and stays with me as long as he can to protect me. I also get behind the bed and stay quiet until the wind blows by.

Thanks to Dad, as I get older, I am learning to not be so afraid of the wind when it blows hard.

The Lazy Girl

I get to be in the house and sleep inside at night, but I don't get to be up on all the furniture.

I am allowed to be on my Lazy Girl recliner, though. I love my Lazy Girl. It is very comfy.

The only problem is that I am nearly full grown now, and I am almost too big for it. So what I usually do is sleep all curled up in a ball or sprawled all over the recliner with my legs, paws, and head hanging off the recliner.

Then when I get a little cramped up or uncomfortable, I get down and stretch out on the floor.

Dad says I am a very long, tall drink of water.

Smokey

Smokey is a big black stuffed bear that gets to be on the new couch all the time. One day last winter, Dad went out for a while and I got to stay in the house. It was just me and Smokey.

There was a blizzard outside and the wind was blowing hard. Like I said before, I don't like the wind; it scares me. I got scared so I got up on the couch with Smokey so we could protect each other from the big bad wind.

Smokey didn't like that I was up on the couch. He told me I had to get down because I wasn't allowed on the new couch. That made me mad, and before I knew what happened, I bit his little black plastic nose off.

I got worried, so I hid his nose under one of the pillows on the couch and got down and went behind my Lazy Girl to get away from the wind.

A long time later, Dad came home. It wasn't until the next day that he realized that Smokey was missing his nose. He found it under the pillow on the couch. There was some dog hair on the couch so Dad figured out that I had been on the couch and had bitten Smokey's nose off.

It sure is hard to get away with anything around here.

Identity Theft

Two-leggeds know who they are because they have birth certificates, driver's licenses, and Social Security cards, but dogs have only their collars.

My collar has my name tag with my name, phone number, and email address. It also has my county dog license and rabies tag on it.

My collar gives me a lot of security; it tells me and others who I am and that I belong to Dad.

When Dad takes my collar off to change tags or give me a new or bigger collar, I hide under the table for protection and safety. Without my collar, I lose my security and my sense of who I am. It can be traumatic for me.

Then Dad puts my collar back on, and just like that, I am Cookie again.

I have told Dad that when he takes off my collar, I should turn him in for identity theft.

The Three Rs

It is said that dogs can learn a vocabulary of up to several hundred human words. I know quite a few myself, like "sit," "stay," "come," "shake," and "heel." But more than just command words, I know other words too, like "squeaker," "scoobie," "dinner," and "walk."

I got so good at learning words that when Dad slips up and says one by accident, I get excited and expect whatever that word meant.

Dad decided that he would spell words out instead. But that didn't work because I can spell too. For instance, when Dad says G-O, I know that spells "go," and when he spells W-A-L-K, I know that Dad is going to take me on a walk. Also, I know that "supper" is spelled S-U-P-P-E-R, and that means I will get my dinner soon.

But that isn't all. I can understand sentences too. When Dad says, "Cookie, go get your squeaker," I know what he wants me to do, and I go get my Smurf or my Dino. And when Dad says, "Cookie, put your sock back in your toy box," I know he wants me to put my sock back where it belongs. I can do that when I want to (which is only some of the time). But my favorite is, "Cookie, go get in the truck," because that means I am going to go for a walk at the park.

All in all, I think I am pretty intelligent and communicate well with Dad. In fact, that's how I came to tell Dad to write this book.

Camping

Dad says the object of camping is to see how dirty you can get. But that is okay because we always camp near water, so cleaning up is easy. We camp near the river, along a creek, or at the lake. That way we can go swimming or take the canoe out too.

We camp in a tent and sleep on the ground in sleeping bags. In the tent, I sleep next to Dad, just like I do at home.

After a full day of hiking and swimming, we are pretty tired. We have a campfire every night. The smoke chases us all around the fire ring. Dad hasn't learned yet to lay on the ground below the fire so the rising smoke doesn't ever bother you. I will have to work on that with him this summer.

Dad stays up pretty late, sitting around the campfire, roasting marshmallows, and gazing at stars like the Big Dipper and the Milky Way. Some of the stars even tumble out of the sky, falling with a fiery tail.

After a while, I get really tired, so I usually go into the tent and get my spot for the night on the sleeping bag.

In the morning, I am first to wake up. If the rain fly isn't on the tent and the windows are zipped down, I just sit up in the tent and listen to the early morning sounds and watch the birds, waiting for Dad to wake up.

After a few days of camping, we are glad to get back home and sleep in our bed. Camping is so much fun, but it really wears you out. When we get home, I usually just lay outside on the cool green grass and dream about my adventures and about our next camping trip.

The Beaver Pond

The beaver pond is my favorite place in the whole world. It's where I learned to swim.

The beaver pond is a one-mile hike from where we park our ol' black truck at the park. Cottonwood Grove is a mile up the canyon beyond the beaver pond.

Dad and I go to the beaver pond almost every day. Sometimes, we just go as far as the pond and spend our time there. Other times, we go past the beaver pond on up the canyon to Cottonwood Grove. On those days, I get two visits to the beaver pond: one on the way up and one on the way back.

My best friend Joe Beaver lives at the beaver pond. It was his family that dammed up the creek and built the pond.

Lots of other animals live at the pond or visit it too, like the deer, coyotes, owls, ducks, woodpeckers, quail, frogs, and even rattlesnakes.

In summer, Dad and I swim in the pond every day. I usually start my swimming season in March and swim all the way until the pond freezes over. Dad doesn't have a warm coat like me, so his swim season is shorter and doesn't start until late April, but he also swims right up until the pond freezes over. Some years, we swim until almost Thanksgiving.

In winter, when the pond freezes over, Dad ice skates and chases a hockey puck around the pond with his hockey stick. It's fun for me to slide around on the ice, exploring and chasing after Dad.

I just can't get enough of the beaver pond.

The Penalty Box

In the winter, Joe Beaver lets Dad and me skate on his pond and play pond hockey.

Skating was an adventure for me that first season. I was sliding and sprawling all over the ice, just like Bambi. By the middle of the winter, though, I had my skates on my paws too.

Dad would skate all over the pond and really fast too. I would run behind him and then cut in front of him, making him turn off and sometimes nearly fall. It was a lot of fun.

One time, while I was exploring off the ice near the edge of the pond, Dad skated clear over to the other side of the pond. I hit the ice running and charged up behind Dad. Then I cut his legs out from under him, and he hit the ice hard.

Dad said, "In the NHL, if that had been a real hockey game, you would have been given two minutes in the penalty box for tripping."

Beaver-Timberrrr

Joe Beaver is my best friend at the pond; he has a lodge built right on the water.

We don't get to see Joe very often, but he does leave signs for us to see. He leaves lots of teeth marks on tree stumps and big piles of wood chips wherever he falls trees. Sometimes we even see bark that he strips off of branches.

When Dad and I do see Joe Beaver, he slaps his tail hard on the surface of the water to let us know that he sees us.

Joe likes to play tricks on me and Dad too. Several times, he has dropped a tree right across the trail we take when we hike up to Cottonwood Grove. When we hear a loud crack and the thunderous thud of a tree hitting the ground, we know that Joe has just cut down another tree.

The best trick Joe Beaver ever played on me and Dad was right at the Beaver Pond. We were there swimming when I heard something rustling in the bushes at the edge of the pond. I was on high alert for a bird or maybe a deer.

At least that was what we both thought, until all of a sudden, a big aspen tree began cracking and fell right into the pond, splashing us with water. That tree landed pretty close to us.

Dad and I were sure that Joe got a big chuckle out of that; he was probably bent over in laughter when he saw us paddle our way back to the other side of the pond.

He probably yelled, "Timberrr," as he fell that aspen; we just didn't hear him.

Woodsy Owl

Great Horned Owl carving

Dad and I were swimming at the beaver pond; I was in the water near the dam when I heard something in the bushes. I had never seen anything like it before. Of course, Dad was oblivious to it until he saw me pointing. Then he looked and said, "It's a Great Horned Owl."

Dad said that the owl was either sick or had a wounded wing because he just sat there, motionless. We moved in closer, and he tried to fly but couldn't, so we let him scamper off, and we went about our daily swim.

On the way out, I sniffed the owl out again; he was upstream from the pond, sitting on a log. Dad and I approached slowly and got within an arm's length of him. You would not believe the size of those big yellow eyes; they were as big as saucers. They were huge metallic discs ... just beautiful.

When Dad saw his bright and alert eyes, he knew that the owl wasn't sick but had a wounded wing. We just stayed there a few minutes watching Woodsy and then slowly walked away. That day and night, we prayed that Woodsy's wing would heal so that he could hunt for food again and survive.

We never saw Woodsy again but we will never forget him.

Quail-Flushing

For a dog like me, there is no better place to be than at the park. It's just a big ol' birdcage for all of my feathered friends.

There's hawks and eagles and owls; there's bluebirds and orioles and tanagers; there's larks and chukar and doves; there's ducks and geese and wild turkeys; there's kingfishers and woodpeckers and hummingbirds. The list of my feathered friends at the park goes on and on … it's just an awesome aviary.

But my favorite feathered friend and the one I have the most fun with is the California Quail. They hang out in large coveys in the bush, and I have to be on the alert for them always, especially when Dad and I hike up the canyon. When I hear them, I point and then move in slowly until they flush out in every direction. If I haven't pointed them out, and they sense danger, they will unexpectedly fly out of the bush in a flurry of feathers and scatter everywhere. If Dad and I aren't expecting it, they can make us jump out of our skin. Quail are exciting and thrilling birds. They keep me alert and sharpen my senses.

Bald Eagle

I always see my friend the Bald Eagle when we go to the lake. He sits atop the old snag across from our favorite cove. I watch him soaring high and diving down to catch fish, and I wish I could fly.

We get to the lake early in the morning and I retrieve my frisbee for Dad. Dad says he sees the eagle watching me too. He says that if the eagle could talk, he would say this: "I see Cookie shred and power through the water, and I wish I could swim."

So I think if I could fly and if the eagle could swim, we would rule the skies and the seas; we would be "bald retrievers."

Dog Town Yacht Club

There's a yacht club in Richmond, Virginia, called Dog Town Yacht Club. Most yacht clubs have their own flag, or burgee, and members fly them on their yachts and boats. Dog town flies a triangular flag that is white with a red disc at the hoist. In the red disc is a silhouette of the head of a black Labrador retriever.

Dad and I thought it was so cool that there's a yacht club that has a burgee with my head on it. We joined the club, and Dad signed up under my name, Cookie Smith. There are three of us Labradors who are members: me, Goose, and Danny.

That's not all. We ordered a burgee from Dog Town and hung it on the wall at home under my picture. Not every dog can say they have their mug on a yacht club flag.

I think me and Goose and Danny should get together and have a retrieving regatta.

Baywatch

Dad trained me to pull him through the water while he has hold of my tail. I am good at pulling that kind of weight through the water.

Dad says that if someone is stranded in the water, I could pull them safely back to shore. He says that is a real lifesaving skill and that I could qualify for a job with *Baywatch*.

Baywatch–Feather River

It was like any other day at the beach: The sun was hot, and the water was cool.

We arrived early, and I got my lifesaving recertification by pulling Dad across the river and back. By noon, there were a hundred people on the beach; most were young college kids.

It was my day as beach life-dog. Besides keeping an eye on all the kids at the beach and floating in the river, my main concern was the long rope swing across the river. When the kids drop off the rope into the river, they are about fifteen feet above the water, so it takes a few seconds for them to resurface after they hit the water.

Some of the kids were very acrobatic off the rope, doing double back flips, dives, can openers, and even cannonballs.

Just to be safe, whenever someone went off the rope swing, I swam out toward the rope to stand by, in case a rescue was necessary. When they resurfaced and began swimming back to shore, I knew they were safe and would swim back to Dad and watch for the next one to take a swing.

There were a hundred people at Pulga Beach that day. The next day was Labor Day, and we heard there were over a thousand people on the beach. I bet there had to be at least ten beach life-dogs that day.

Walking on Water

All aboard Cookie's canoe

Dad and I go to the lake often during spring and summer.

He built a plywood platform for me to sit on that slips over the bow of the canoe. This is where I ride when we paddle out into the lake.

Sometimes, I get restless and impatient and don't sit still, like I'm supposed to. At times like this, I often fall into the lake.

Then I have to swim next to the canoe until Dad is able to paddle back to shore, and I can remount on my platform.

Needless to say, I have done lots of long-distance swims like this. I even had to swim halfway across the lake a few times. LOL.

One summer day we were gliding very quietly across the lake, about a hundred yards offshore. I was sitting pretty at the very tip of the bow, like a ship ornament. I think my form was silhouetted against the sun.

Anyway, we saw some guy on the shore look up and heard him say to his friend, "Hey, look, there's a dog walking across the water."

Dad cracked up laughing and said he thought that guy had way too much sun and maybe too much beer as well.

River Otters

Little Joe Beaver has always told me that Oregon (the Beaver State) is a special place for beavers, otters, and other animals. He said that the Oregon state flag even has a beaver on one side. He told me that I needed to make at least one trip to the holy land.

Dad took me with him when he went up to visit the Oregon coast. Along the road, there was a nice little lake, and he stopped to let me stretch out and take care of my chores. I retrieved a stick for Dad quite a few times. We both liked this little lake and went back every day.

On our third visit to the little lake, I saw four River Otters. They were across the lake playing in the water and catching fish. They love to swim as much as I do. I just sat there, watching them diving and rolling in the water, and when I was retrieving, they were watching me too. We were all very curious about each other.

Later, curiosity got the best of the otters, and they came swimming toward me; they seemed to be inviting me to join them in the water. When they got really close, I couldn't resist any longer. I jumped in and swam toward them.

The mother otter stayed back and let her young ones come see just what this big black otter-dog was all about. They swam all around me, diving and swimming under me and sliding across my fur. It was all very playful, and we sniffed each other. For those few moments, we had a great time together in the water, just swimming for joy. Then the mother told her young ones to come back across the lake. She said goodbye to me as they all swam off.

Needless to say, Dad was very anxious as he watched all this. He said it was very dangerous because just one otter could easily take down a dog in the water. He said I was very lucky to have had this experience and even more lucky to have lived to tell about it. He said the otters could have considered me a threat and attacked me.

Even so, I will always remember my swim with the otters and that the mother otter told me I am a great swimmer.

Quail-Jaws

Dad says that the measure of a great retrieving dog is how soft their mouth is because a hunter wants his dog to retrieve the game but not damage it.

Dad and I were out in the park the other day, and I sniffed and pointed some quail in the brush. I jumped and pounced where the quail were, and they flushed out of the brush in a flurry of feathers. It was an explosion of birds, but there were some that hadn't been flushed yet. I had them spotted and jumped really high toward them, and just at that instant, a bunch of the young birds burst out from right under me. While I was hanging in the air, one of the young quail flew right into my mouth. I had it in my grasp … he was mine.

But before my paws hit the ground, I released the young quail, and he fluttered off without missing a wing beat. It all happened in just an instant, but Dad said it was the most athletic display of canine acrobatics he had ever seen. Without a doubt, he said there was not another dog with a mouth as soft as mine.

Woodrat

One day, Dad and I went up to Cottonwood Grove. On our way back, I sniffed something down the hill and ran off the trail.

It was one of those times I was successful at hunting. I heard something in the rocks and went after it. I came out with a Woodrat that I had caught by the back of the neck.

That was my prey and my prize. I was going to protect it, even from Dad. He tried and tried to get it from me, but I wouldn't give it up. He was worried that I might eat that rat.

Dad was proud of me for having the skills to capture my prey but said that as far as feed goes, I am a Purina girl.

Hornets

One time we went camping, but all of our favorite campgrounds were full. So we went back off the road along a creek and found a good place to set up camp.

We have to be near water so we can swim or at least get wet. It was the middle of summer, so the creek was pretty low.

We had to hike a little ways from the tent to get to water. We had to make our way through the brush and cross some logs.

I was leading the way when I heard a noise near the ground. We were at the swimming hole, so I sniffed it out. That was a big mistake because as soon as I put my nose to the ground, the place exploded in a wild buzzing of mad hornets. They were everywhere, and they were after us. We scattered like flies; luckily, no one got stung.

After the hornets settled back into their nest, we got wet in the creek but stayed clear of their nest. We left them alone, and they left us alone.

The greatest thing about camping is that it is such an adventure.

Rattlesnake

Every year, Dad and I see four or five rattlesnakes while on our adventures in the park. Dad taught me about snakes when I was a little pup. He taught me to be alert for them and to give them lots of space, not just rattlesnakes but even gopher and garter snakes.

Sometimes, rattlesnakes lay in the grass or in leaves and debris along the trail. It can be hard to see them.

One day, we swam across the pond and went walking in the grass on the other side. Dad was ahead of me; I heard something move in the grass, so I went ahead of him. Then I froze in my tracks and pointed. Dad asked, "What is it, Cookie?"

After a few seconds of staring into the grass, a Diamondback Rattlesnake came into focus; it was coiled up in the grass right in our path and ready to strike. Dad said it was time to shake, rattle, and roll.

Dad made the grass shake, the snake rattled his tail, and we rolled on out of there fast.

Blackberry Bramble

One day while we were at the river, I was retrieving sticks for Dad. I decided to spice things up a bit so I started dropping the sticks in the blackberry bushes after I retrieved them.

It was hilarious watching Dad tip-toe barefoot through the brambles and singing out as he was pricked and poked by the thorns. It was all in good fun, and later, we all had a great laugh at Dad's expense.

The blackberries were sweet and delightful, but the brambles were very sharp and painful.

Fried Chicken

One spring day we drove over to Table Mountain to see the wildflowers and waterfalls. That night, we stayed over in a pet-friendly motel. For dinner, Dad brought back a bucket of fried chicken. The smell of that chicken drove me wild all night.

The next day we packed up and headed back home. Dad put the box with the fried chicken in the back of the Jeep. Along the way, he was sightseeing and looking for photos. I couldn't take it anymore. My nose got the best of me.

As slick as I could, I retrieved both of the chicken breasts from the box and gobbled them down as fast as I could. They were paw-licking good.

Later, Dad stopped at a nice spot along the Feather River. He said he wanted a snack and went for the chicken. "It's all gone!" he yelled out.

I looked as innocent as I could with my big brown puppy dog eyes, but he knew it was me that took the chicken. I was caught red-pawed.

Table Mountain

In February, we are usually still frozen in the grip of winter at home. That's when Dad and I take a trip to Table Mountain, a place over in the valley where spring comes early.

At Table Mountain, there are hundreds of acres of spring wildflowers in bloom, like owl's clover, golden poppies, and lupine. There are several waterfalls full and flowing, and the whole area is dotted with stately old oak trees that stand tall, like rangers watching over a park.

There is nothing like running through vernal pools of flowers; it's like being splashed with a cannonade of color.

There is nothing like swimming in a bubbling pool of cool water at the bottom of a waterfall; it's like relaxing in a canine spa.

Retrieving gnarly old oak branches under falling water is a very exciting and totally drenching experience.

We love our midwinter escapes to Table Mountain; they get us thinking about springtime at the beaver pond.

Blackie

Blackie ready for his apple and carrot treats

We love to visit our good friend Blackie; he's a big ol' black donkey that lives on Cherokee Road, near Table Mountain. We always bring a big bag of carrots and some apples when we visit him.

We will park along the side of the road and start calling his name. In no time, he starts braying and comes running to the fence. He will put his head over the fence, anxiously waiting for his carrots and apples.

While he is eating his treats, he lets Dad rub and scratch his head and ears. Sometimes, he starts braying again while he gets his scratching.

It's hard to say goodbye to Blackie. But when we do, we watch him walk slowly back into his meadow and start grazing again.

We sure do love our Blackie.

Dog Tired

I am proud to say that in my puppy days, not once did I gnaw on any furniture or rip up any shoes or clothes, and I never tore out any plants or did any digging in the yard.

This was all because Dad worked me hard, day after day, every day, until I was dog tired.

After long hikes and endless swimming and retrieving, all I wanted to do when I got home was eat and sleep. Then when I woke up the next day, I was fully charged and ready for another day of adventure.

It just goes to prove that a tired dog is a happy dog, and I am a very happy dog.

Firewood

I get to sleep on the bed with Mom and Dad. Mom and I sleep pretty hard and many nights we have a good loud snore-off. We can really saw some logs.

Poor old Dad; he nudges whichever one of us is snoring to stop us, only to have the other one start. On and on this goes, sometimes for hours or even throughout the night.

Who says girls can't cut firewood?

Dad says that me and Mom can easily put up a cord of firewood a night.

River Run

By the summer of my second year, I had become a very strong and powerful swimmer with endless endurance.

One late summer day, Dad, his son, and I boarded the canoe. I rode atop the bow, sitting on the wooden platform Dad made me. We put into the river for a long drift downstream of about seven miles.

Not long after we set off, I jumped off the canoe and went into the river and started swimming alongside of Dad. I felt good that day, and Dad let me keep swimming in the river.

Before we knew it, we had drifted over a mile, and I was still in the water. We encountered all kinds of water: slow-moving, fast-moving, and calm sections of the river.

There were tons of people in the water and on shore. They all watched, with great interest, as I swam along next to the canoe. I heard some say how impressed they were with my swimming ability.

As we drifted downriver and the miles added up, I powered through the calm water, drifted effortlessly in the current, glided smoothly through riffles, and was swept along in the rapids.

For three hours and seven miles, I had not touched bottom, not even one time.

Finally, we hauled out of the water at a bar and grill overlooking the river.

I was a tired dog with a voracious appetite. Dad ordered me a double cheeseburger, and I inhaled the whole thing.

It was a great day of long-distance swimming. I slept next to Dad in the ol' black truck all the way back home.

I was pretty stiff the next day.

I'm gonna remember my river run for a long time. It may have been the greatest day of swimming in my entire life.

The Legend

Since the time I was a pup, Dad has told me the great legend about how man and dog became best friends.

The legend, passed on anonymously, goes like this: After Adam and Eve were banished from Paradise, a huge chasm slowly opened, separating them from the rest of the Animal Kingdom.

But at the very last instant, just before the yawning abyss became too wide, the Dog leaped across the chasm, choosing to spend the rest of his eternity with his friend, Man.

God spelled backwards is Dog!

That's why Dad and I know this legend is true.

PART TWO

Polar Bear

Dad isn't as lucky as me when it comes to swimming gear. I have a nice dense, flat, and oily coat of fur that sheds water and insulates me like a wetsuit.

I have big ol' webbed feet that Dad calls swimming fins. When I spread them out wide, I can really power through the water.

But poor old Dad. He has no wetsuit and no swimming fins. All he has is his birthday suit.

But I give him a lot of credit. He gets in the water in April when the beaver pond is filled with ice-cold snow-melted water. That water takes his breath away when he first gets in, and it turns him red and makes him numb all over.

We swim all spring and summer. When fall comes, the pond water starts getting cold again. Dad can tough it out until the leaves fall from their trees.

Soon after that, our swimming season is over because the beaver pond freezes over.

Dad says he loves cold water. I think he is a polar bear.

Jack Frost

Figure 8 skated on the frozen beaver pond

Joe Beaver is my best friend in summer because he is the one who builds the pond that me and Dad swim in.

Jack Frost is my best friend in winter because he is the one who freezes our pond and turns it into a skating rink.

When the pond is frozen crystal clear and the ice is as smooth as glass, skating conditions are perfect.

Dad laces up his hockey skates and carves figure 8s onto the surface of the pond. This roughs up the ice and gives me some traction to race across the pond.

As long as the skies stay clear and cold, and Jack Frost keeps blowing his below-zero breath over the pond, we were able to slide and glide across the ice.

But when it snows, things change. Pine cones and needles and grit get embedded into the ice. Ruts appear, and skating becomes a rough and bumpy ride.

We have to wait for the sun to melt snow off of the pond and for Jack Frost to refreeze our rink.

Friction

Dad has noticed that during the summer months, my chest is nearly bald. He says this is because I swim so much and so hard that the friction of me powering through the water wears thin the hair on my underside.

Not to worry, though; during the winter, when swimming is over for the year, my hair recovers and grows back.

Physics

Dad says I passed my physics class.

When I am swimming and retrieving in the beaver pond, I have to make my way through a maze of obstacles to get back to Dad with my stick.

Sometimes, I have to adjust the length of my stick by gripping it closer to one side or the other so I can get past narrow gaps between snags or rocks.

Also, I have an old pull sock, which is two socks tied together in the middle. Dad and I play tug-of-war with this long sock.

If I pull straight against Dad, he can overpower me pretty easy. When I pull down on the sock as well as against Dad, I can get him off-balance and overpower him and win the tug-of-war.

Physics is my favorite class, and I'm gonna take it again next year.

First Impression

When we met Mom, we greeted her at the front gate. It was raining so we were both wet.

Dad had his old rain gear on and after he greeted Mom with a big hug, she said, "Wow, you smell like a wet dog."

All I could think to myself was, *Way to go, Dad. You smell more like a dog than I do.*

Jack Rabbit

I was carrying my retrieving stick as we walked across the sand dunes. It had been a great morning of retrieving in the river.

Just ahead, I spotted a pair of very long, black-tipped ears twitching back and forth. They seemed to be very alert and scanning for any sign of danger. As I walked closer, the brush atop the dune exploded in a flash of leaping legs that covered ten feet with each stride.

I took off chasing this bounding creature. Whatever it was, it changed direction with each long leap, and I was soon left in the dust. All I could see was a big white underside of a tail, waving in the breeze like some sort of warning flag.

By now, Dad was blowing his safety whistle to let me know I needed to return to him. I had been completely fooled and out-matched, so I gave up the chase and returned to him.

When I got back, Mom and Dad both laughed wildly and said that I had met my match in the form of a Black-tailed Jack Rabbit.

Sea Otter-Surfing

Just like river otters in Oregon, a Sea Otter up on the Olympic Peninsula in Washington invited me into the surf for a playful swim. He did everything he could to get me into the ocean water: diving and rolling and getting so close that we almost came nose to nose.

Dad didn't let me go out and play. He said that even though it was obvious that me and otters have a kinship, the ocean was just too big, and I would be out of my element and at a real disadvantage. There could have been a real problem.

But we both had a lot of fun watching the sea otter doing all his playful antics in the surf.

Bullfrog

I have hunted mice and gophers most of my life and bagged my share. But now I am getting interested in fishing too.

In the spring at the beaver pond and some other nearby ponds, Bullfrogs are very active. My mouth is watering for a nice juicy pair of frog legs. I want to know if they really taste like chicken.

Lately, I have been shredding water in the ponds, trying to catch my first frog. It's really hard because they croak to get your attention, but then just when you're ready to pounce on them, they dive underwater and swim off. Then they surface behind you and croak at you again.

My dad says it is hilarious watching me fish for frogs. He says that it's like the running of the bulls. Bullfrogs, that is.

Merganser

Dad and I were soaking in the cool water of the beaver pond early one July morning when all of a sudden, out of nowhere, a Common Merganser duck landed on the pond, just a few feet from us.

He was a beauty with his white body, bright green head, and red bill. He floated around the pond like we weren't even there. We stayed motionless in the water, watching him. After he drifted down toward the end of the pond, he dove down and came up in another place.

I swam back to shore on the other side of the pond, and it didn't even disturb the merganser; he just kept floating and diving. I even crashed into the pond to retrieve a stick for Dad, and he still paid us no attention. He was diving, and that was it.

Dad said we should have put a red "Diver Down" flag out for the merganser.

I told Dad I wanted to learn to dive like that duck, and he said, "Well then, we better get you some scuba gear."

The Dog Father

Dad's last job was Director of Animal Control at a dog and livestock shelter up on the north coast.

This was a high-kill shelter when Dad took over.

Dad got the county Board of Supervisors to pass an administrative policy that prohibited adoptable or treatable dogs from being destroyed.

He also began working with the local Humane Society and lots of animal rescue organizations and dedicated individuals all over the United States.

Dad was able to save the lives of hundreds of animals. He saved the lives of old dogs, sick dogs, blind dogs, crippled dogs, mentally challenged dogs, behaviorly challenged dogs, starving horses, and nearly every animal that entered his shelter.

There were thirty-two dog kennels at the shelter, and we lived in a small trailer right next to them. We light-heartedly said that we lived in Kennel #33.

The dogs at the shelter thought of my dad as their Pound Daddy, but to me he was more than that; he was the Dog Father.

I am really proud of my dad for caring so much about neglected and abused dogs and livestock and for finding good homes for them and saving their lives.

Deputy Dog

Sometimes when Dad transports dogs to a rescue organization, he takes me with him. He deputizes me and lets me ride shotgun. It is a very important job; I have to keep Dad focused on driving and paying attention to the road.

One time, we were driving dogs through southern Oregon when a state trooper pulled in behind us with his lights flashing. Dad had been daydreaming and driving too fast.

The trooper asked Dad if he knew why he pulled him over. Dad said it was probably for speeding. Then the trooper asked Dad if he knew how fast he was going. Dad guessed and said about forty-six miles per hour. The trooper informed Dad that he had been clocked at fifty-eight miles per hour in an area posted for forty-five miles per hour.

About the time the trooper asked to see Dad's driver's license, the puppies in the back of the pickup began whining, and I threw my head back against the headrest with my big sad eyes, looking right at that trooper.

Dad told the trooper that he was transporting shelter dogs to a rescue. It didn't take the trooper long after seeing my big sad eyes and hearing the puppies crying to say to Dad, "Tell you what, Mr. Smith, I am going let you go with a warning this time, but pay more attention while you are driving."

After we were back on the road, Dad breathed a big sigh of relief and told me I had really earned my wages and done my job as a deputy dog.

I said, "It was nothing, Dad; all I had to do was use my feminine canine charm and flash my big brown eyes, and that trooper melted like butter."

Parvo Pups

Before Dad became Director of Animal Control, any dog at the shelter that came down with the parvo virus was destroyed immediately.

Dad changed all of that. He consulted with the local veterinarian about treating parvo dogs, most of whom were puppies. Soon, dogs were being saved.

The first dog Dad saved from the parvo virus was a Labrador retriever pup named River.

Dad isolated River into a space warmed with a heat lamp. He was given disposable blankets to lay on. Dad forced Pedialite down River to hydrate him. The vet prescribed injectable meds, and Dad administered them twice a day.

His space had to be cleaned and disinfected a couple times a day. Dad plugged a radio in for River and tuned it to play softly so he didn't feel lonely. He visited him throughout the day and night to monitor his progress.

The long treatment lasted ten days. The first few nights, Dad was up every two hours, checking on and caring for River. As soon as River tested negative for the parvo virus, he was put back into the general population at the shelter.

Not long after that, River was adopted into a good home.

Over the next five years, Dad and Mom saved over 80 percent of the dogs at the shelter that were infected with the parvo virus.

It was a new era at the shelter.

Event Staff

I'm not saying I'm spoiled or anything, but I have an event staff that cleans up after me.

I mean Dad picks up my droppings every day off the lawn to keep things sanitary.

My toys are kept in a wicker basket in the living room.

Some evenings, I play with all of my toys, including two squeakers, three or four pull socks, and a couple of balls. Sometimes, I have toys scattered all over the living room and throughout the house. But not to worry; Dad picks them all up and puts them away in my toy box.

Sometimes, I like to raid the dirty clothes hamper (duck pond) and drag out socks (ducks) and scatter them all over the house. Of course, Dad picks them up too.

Dad has tried to train me to put my toys away when I am done playing with them. I put things back once in a while, but I do better when he tells me to go get a toy to play with.

Computer Dog

Dad says everybody's gotta get the latest computer: the one with the fastest processor, the most memory, and the best software.

He says it's impossible to keep up ... unless you get one with a K-9 processor and all-dog software.

That's right. I have a nose that's many times more sensitive than Dad's. Now that's a processor that can't be beat.

My memory is limitless.

Add to this my visual and hearing software package, and you have the greatest computer system God ever designed.

I'm equipped with a rechargeable, wireless canine power source and plenty of playful mega bites.

To download and print documents, I just tell Dad the information and he writes it down on the pages of this book.

My whole system comes with a lifetime guarantee. And best of all, Dad says I'm very user friendly and have laptop capability.

I'm the whole package, a real computer dog.

Hideaway

I have some favorite places in our house where I like to go to be by myself or to feel safe.

I like to get behind my Lazy Girl chair in the corner of the living room. I like to get under the desk in the computer room, and I like to get under the dining room table.

I enjoy being by myself when I escape to my hideaways.

Mom can pet me when I am hidden away, but I don't let Dad pet me. So Dad jokes and says that these hideaways are for girls only, and no boys are allowed.

Beachcombing

Dad is a real beachcomber; he loves to walk along the ocean, looking for sand dollars, sea stars, sea glass, and nautical stuff.

While he does that, I explore the beach myself, looking for my own canine ocean treasures to retrieve, like driftwood and, best of all, tennis balls.

I'm a real hound with a nose for finding tennis balls. I have found dozens of them. Some of my prize discoveries include a ball that glows in the dark, one that has XXX stamped on it, and one that says "Air Dog." That one has a squeaker in it too.

When I find a ball at the ocean, I like to carry it up the beach and then let it roll down into the surf. Then I race after it and bring it back up the beach again. Sometimes, Dad throws the tennis ball for me, and I tear up the sand as I race to retrieve it.

Just like Dad, I love beachcombing too.

Beaver-Stick Maker

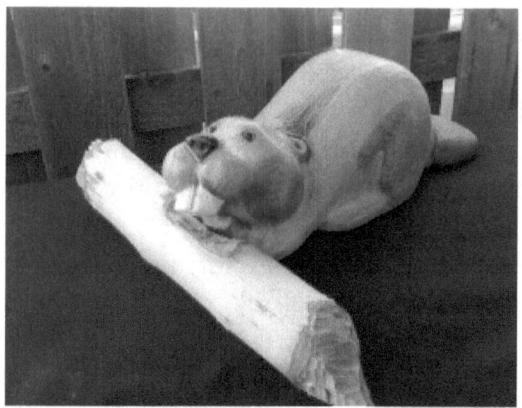

Beaver carving

Retrieving sticks is an important and necessary skill for Labrador retrievers. The sticks must meet a strict set of specifications to provide the best results and long-lasting performance.

I have my retrieving sticks custom made. They are crafted from fine aspen or alder wood. They are whittled on the ends and cut to lengths that are perfect for throwing and retrieving: neither too long nor too short. The workmanship given to my sticks is of the very highest quality.

My sticks are milled at night or in the early morning hours and are available for pickup near the beaver pond or the creek.

One of my best friends cuts and finishes my retrieving sticks for me; his whole family is in the business. They have been cutting and crafting sticks forever.

My stick maker is Joe Beaver.

Fox

Dad and I were on our way back from the beaver pond and had just passed the substation on the gravel road. I saw a really big gray squirrel with a bushy tail and chased him up an oak tree. Just then, Dad and I heard this really loud and scary barking and growling noise. It continued and sounded like some sort of emergency warning.

Dad looked over to the side of the oak tree and saw the vixen who was sounding her alarm. It turned out that the big gray squirrel I had chased up the oak tree was not a squirrel after all but a baby fox, and his mother was warning us to stay away from her pup.

Dad saw the little baby fox climbing higher into the oak to hide from us. He had a gray coat, and his eyes were big as saucers; he must have been scared to be away from his mom.

Mom was smaller than the males we have seen at the park, but her coat was also gray on top, with beautiful red fur underneath. She was very protective of her pup and kept making that loud barking and growling noise, so we heeded her warning and just left the two of them alone.

Dad says that the Gray Fox is the only canine species that has real tree-climbing skills; that little fox sure did scamper up the oak tree as fast as any squirrel.

Squirrel

Chickaree, dickory, dock, the Pine Squirrel—also known as a chickaree—ran up the clock (well, he ran up the tree, anyway).

That's right. Dad and I were swimming at the beaver pond when we heard a ruckus in the bushes … lots of noisy trills. I swam back across the pond to go investigate. As I bolted out of the water, the chickaree scampered up the cottonwood tree and raced along the branches, jumping from tree to tree. He made it to the safety of his summer nest, amidst a middens of shredded pine cones.

I stood up with my front paws on the cottonwood tree trunk and watched his every move. The chickaree just peered down at me and chattered loudly back as if to say, "Get thee back, you brute!"

I never saw such a good climber; that squirrel could jump from tree to tree better than anyone. It made me wish I could climb trees and swing from branch to branch too. If I could, I would pound my chest with my paws and bark out that I was lord of the jungle, just like Tarzan.

Critter Gitter

Going out every day with Dad on an adventure has really awakened that ancient canine call of the wild, that primal instinct and urge to hunt that lays latent in all dogs.

I'm keen to every sign of prey, like the sound of a gopher underground or the slightest rustling of the grass as a mouse moves under cover.

Like a coyote or a fox, I freeze motionless: my tail outstretched, paw held up, and nose and eyes pointed. Then leaping high and forward, I grab that mouse or dig up that gopher and shake them till they are limp and motionless, just like my ancestor the wolf did.

Dad says if I ever got separated from him and escaped the coyotes and mountain lions, I could feed myself until I found my way back to him. He says I am a real "critter-gitter."

The Statue of Liberty

Dad says that the Statue of Liberty sits in New York Harbor to greet all those who sail by on their way into the United States.

Dad and I swim at the beaver pond nearly two hundred days a year. On occasion, something will spook me while we are swimming. It could be an unexpected gunshot, my sense that a lion or bear is nearby, or perhaps some less-than-friendly dogs making their way to the pond for a drink who growl menacingly when they see us.

At these times, I like to stay close to Dad for protection. When he is in the pond, this means that I must swim out to him. I will swim right to him and climb up with my paws resting over his shoulders. He supports my back legs as he stands in the middle of the pond. I tower over the pond with a wide view of all that I survey.

This makes for quite a sight. Dad says that though we are not the Statue of Liberty, we could be called the Statue of Friendship, set in the pond to greet all those canines and humans who make their way through the park.

Cornucopia

Dad plants a vegetable garden every year. What I like best about the garden is laying on the grass, just outside the garden gate, and savoring the sweet smell of strawberries in the early morning (and in the evening too).

Sometimes, Dad forgets to close the gate, and I sneak into the garden and head right for the strawberry patch. I pick the sweetest and juiciest-tasting berries I can find—that is, until Dad catches me in the garden and scoots me out. He says he doesn't mind me taking a few berries once in a while, but I wind up making too much strawberry jam with my big old paws, trying to get to the best fruit. So he usually picks two or three for me every day and just hands them to me while I am waiting for him outside the garden gate.

I like green beans too. They grow through the fence, so I can pick them without getting into much trouble. I like how snappy they are, and they taste really good too, crunchy, like my dog food.

Dad grows lots of big pumpkins for the kids and grandkids. They get really big and turn orange at the end of the season. Dad says all their first names are Jack and their last names are O'Lantern; they must be Irish. I don't mess with the pumpkins much 'cause they are just too big and really heavy.

At the end of the growing season, I get to roam through the garden; I like tearing through the rows of corn stalks, especially if there is a cat hiding in there and I can chase it up onto the roof of the garden shed.

Baseball under the Lights

Every once in a while, I like a good old game of baseball. So the other night, around midnight, I decided to get Dad up for a game. He was asleep, so I had to bat at him a bunch of times with my big old paw. Finally, I woke him up and said, "Put me in, Coach, I'm ready to play."

He got up, and I led him out to the living room to my toy box, where all my balls are. I grabbed one of my favorite tennis balls and dropped it for Dad. He turned on the lights, and we had a good game of pepper. He rolled the ball to me, and I grabbed it and threw it back to him; then he would bat it back to me again. We played for a good ten minutes or so.

That was just enough for me to keep myself in playing shape, so we shut the field lights off and headed back to the locker room for a good night's sleep.

Dad laughed and said, "There's nothing like baseball under the lights."

Surfer Girl

I have been to the ocean a few times now. The water tastes icky; it's way too salty for me to drink, but I like to swim in it.

The first time I was at the ocean, I wasn't paying attention, and a wave washed me into the surf, and the next thing I knew, I was swimming.

Dad throws driftwood out for me to retrieve. Sometimes, I have to body-surf out to grab the wood and retrieve it.

Just like in fresh water, I also get waterlogged in the ocean. The salt dries and cakes on my skin, so I have to roll in the sand for ten or fifteen minutes, and then I shake the sand and salt off of me.

I smell like brine for a day or so after swimming in the ocean, but the saltwater does make my coat really shine.

Dad says I am his little surfer girl.

Treasure Trove

Dad bought a whole bag full of tennis balls for Mom's dog LadyBug.

She can chase balls all day; Mom throws the ball down the hill from atop the deck. Occasionally, one gets lost in the brush or high grass, so she needs a big supply of replacement balls on hand.

If the bag of balls isn't put away, LadyBug will find them and try to take them out.

Mom had hidden the bag of balls from LadyBug by burying them in amongst her granddaughter's stuffed animals. They were pretty well hidden on the lower shelf.

Well, being the retriever that I am, I nosed them out pretty easily. Mom was busy in the kitchen and didn't notice what I was doing.

I am also very handy with my paws and mouth, and I managed to open the drawstring on the bag and began taking the balls out one by one and dropping them on the floor.

Mom thought I was just dropping one ball on the floor over and over in an attempt to get her to throw it for me.

Finally, she turned and looked to find that I had emptied the ball bag and had every ball scattered all over the floor. She laughed and then gathered them all up and hid them from me too.

It was a real treasure trove of balls; I had a great time while it lasted.

Mirror Buddies

Mom put a blue bandana in my Christmas stocking this year. It looked really good on me, and I wore it for several days.

One afternoon, a few days after Christmas, I was upstairs in Mom and Dad's room and walked by the mirrored doors.

I was used to seeing myself in those mirrors, but this time, there was another dog looking back at me. She looked like me but had a bandana round her neck. She mimicked every move I made. I barked at her, and she barked back; I nosed her, and she nosed me back; I crouched down and chased at her, and she did too.

I couldn't believe there was another dog in our home, but then Dad reminded me that I was still wearing my new Christmas bandana. When he told me that, it all made sense. That was the first time I was seeing myself wearing it.

I guess even an older dog learns new things once in a while.

Beaver-Slap Happy

Dad had to take me to Dead Lake early because of his work schedule this week.

At the north end of the lake, I was busy shredding my way through the water to retrieve sticks for Dad when we both heard that unmistakable loud slap on the water. It sounded like a boulder thrown into the lake. It was a beaver sounding the alarm, giving us a warning by slapping his tail on the water.

We stood there motionless, watching the beaver slowly swimming toward us and then circling back; he came closer, circled back, and came closer again. Finally, we must have moved because he slapped the water right in front of us, nearly splashing us.

I couldn't take it any longer and leaped into the water in hot pursuit of the beaver. Off we went, me chasing and the beaver going "slap happy" with his tail, smacking the water again and again. He would go underwater, surface somewhere else, and slap the water as I chased after him.

I was nearly across the lake when Dad whistled me back. So back to Dad I swam, and all the while the beaver kept going slap happy.

Elk

Dad and I were hiking across a meadow that soon turned into a swamp. We wound up trekking though water and getting tangled in blackberry vines, but we finally made it across the meadow and started hiking along a row of spruce trees.

After clearing the trees, we looked back, and to our amazement, a big bull Elk was standing motionless in the meadow about fifty yards away, watching us. It was still cool that morning, so steam rose from his nostrils as he breathed. He was muddy from rolling in the meadow, and velvet hung from his big rack of antlers.

Unlike the deer we were used to seeing, he did not bolt and run from us but instead stood his ground, looking very formidable. Then he threw his head back and bugled a whistling song of dominance before he just walked slowly away.

That was the first Wapiti (elk) that Dad and I ever saw, and it was a very impressive sight.

The Raven

> Ah, distinctly I remember it was in the bleak December ...
> Deep into that darkness peering, long I stood there wondering, fearing ...
> So that now, to still the beating of my heart, I stood repeating ...
> Let my heart be still a moment, and this mystery explore ...
> Then this ebony bird beguiling my sad fancy into smiling ...
> And his eyes have all the seeming of a demon's that is dreaming ...
> But the Raven still beguiling all my sad soul into smiling ...
> By that heaven that bends above us, by that God we both adore.
>
> From "The Raven" by Edgar Allan Poe

Yes, it was on a dreary December day that I too met the raven, two of them to be exact, and they were as black as I am.

Dad and I were walking on the beach and came upon a carcass washed ashore; we quickly let it be and walked on by.

No sooner had we walked by than from out of the sky two ravens descended, plumes fluttering in the breeze as they hovered over my head, croaking and "kracking." But not to be so easily run off, I stood up on my hind paws and leaped up at them. They scattered off and circled above, only to descend upon me again with more threatening kracking.

Dad said they were probably defending the carcass that they claimed as their own. He said they saw me as a threat and became aggressive in their defense.

But again, not to be run off without a fight, I leapt at them and sent them flying. Dad said it looked like two flying ravens and one four-legged raven locked in a real beach skirmish.

As we got farther from the carcass, the ravens must have felt they chased us off, so they flew back to their treasure and let us go on our way.

Like Edgar Allan Poe, I too have met The Raven.

Greyhound

Sometimes, when it's hot and we're walking through the sand, it feels good to roll down the dunes on my back. It kind of scratches me.

Dad says the sand works like a brush on my coat, taking out the dead hair and foxtails and cleaning it. He says that's why it feels good to me; it's like getting brushed. I love getting brushed.

Anyway, when I get back on my feet, I've turned from black to gray. Dad says I've turned into a greyhound: "the old gray dog."

I have to go swimming to turn back into a black Labrador retriever again.

Black Stag

I like to find the biggest and most gnarly stick I can and drag it down the trail. The other day, I found one that had lots of spikes on both ends. I grabbed it in the middle and trotted down the trail.

Dad said I looked like a big black stag prancing down the trail with my antlers held high in proud display.

The only problem is that I have a long tail, and Dad says elk don't have those.

Dune Doggie

I love running in the dunes at the far end of Dead Lake. The sand is soft and feels so good on my paws. Charging down the dunes is the most fun because it is easy, and I can glide down the sand, but getting to the top of the dunes is really hard work, especially when the sand is dry. At the top of the dunes, the view is great; you can see the ocean and the mountains.

Dad calls me a real dune-doggie.

Gator

One of my favorite things to do is to lay on the carpet on my back and wiggle around, kicking my legs. It just feels good to rub my coat on the carpet. Dad always gets down on the floor when I do this and plays with me. I kick at him with my back legs and make lots of grunting noises and sometimes even grab his arm with my jaws (not too hard, though).

Dad gets a big laugh out of this and he says that I am just a little black alligator thrashing around on the floor, snapping my big ol' jaws.

Hook, Line, and Sinker

I've been injured only once in my life, and that's really amazing since I am out in the wild with Dad nearly every day.

The one and only time I was hurt wasn't that bad, but it was quite an ordeal.

I was retrieving at Dead Lake with Dad. He had thrown a stick out in the lily pads. I retrieved it easily enough, but when I swam back to shore, I felt something sticking me in my chest. Dad noticed right away; he said I had been hooked by someone's fishing lure that had been snagged in the lily pads.

Dad tried to pull it off me, but the hook had gone through my skin and the barb was sticking out, so I was really stuck. He broke off the fishing line from the lure, and we headed back to the truck.

When we got home, Dad tried to clip the barb of the hook and then pull the lure off me, but since I don't like being messed with, that wasn't going to be easy for him to do.

Dad had a backup plan, though. Since he was the Director of Animal Control, he had one of his officers give me a shot of sedative to slow me down. It didn't do much good though; I am pretty big and strong. After about a half hour and no slowing me down, they had to give me another shot. This time, I was down for the count in just a few minutes. Then Dad was able to clip the barb off the hook and pull the lure off me.

I had absolutely no control of my legs and spent the rest of the day and until two o'clock the next morning sleeping off the sedative.

All because I don't like being messed with. I was good as new and none the worse for wear later that next morning.

Dad took the hooks off the lure, and we hung it up in the house as a reminder of our experience. He says I was caught hook, line, and sinker that day.

A Nose for News

No matter what car I ride in, I sit up front, riding shotgun. After a long drive, Dad says the front windshield has so many nose prints on it that it looks like the front page of the local newspaper.

He laughs and says, "Extra, extra, read all about it in today's special windshield edition of The Noseprint News."

"Extra, extra, fresh off the paws, the latest nose. Read all about it; get yours now!"

The Latest Poop on Capitol Hill

This year, we drove up to the Olympic Peninsula, near Discovery Bay, so that Dad could collect more sea glass.

On the way back, we stopped in Olympia to visit the state capitol. It's atop a hill overlooking the whole city. The grounds are landscaped with trees and grass; it's like a park there.

On my early morning walk around the capitol grounds, I got to run across the grass and take care of chores. Dad laughed and said that now I could get back into the car and mark up the front windshield with my nose prints and tell my readers all about the latest poop on Capitol Hill. LOL.

Rhinestone Girl

Dad and I had the wildest adventure ever when we were at the north end of Dead Lake.

I was busy retrieving in the lily pond when all of a sudden, a torrential hailstorm exploded. The hailstones were as big as marbles. They hit the pond with such force that they turned it into a bubbling fountain.

After swimming through the hail, I sprang out of the pond, plastered with ice. Dad said that I looked like I was wearing a black velvet evening gown beaded with rhinestones. He said I looked very elegant and absolutely stunning.

The last minute of the hailstorm was so intense that Dad had to bend over me with his hands covering his head, to protect us both from the relentless pelting of hail.

When it finally stopped and we were able to begin our trek back to the truck, we looked up to see that the sand dunes were completely covered in a blanket of white.

What an awesome display of the wild power of nature.

Blackberry Delights

It's August on the coast, and blackberries are ripe. Dad is always stopping to pick 'em. He says they're really sweet and bursting with goodness. He says it's like sipping cabernet on the vine.

Blackberries are full of vitamins like A and C and something called antioxidants that keep you from getting sick.

Since blackberries are so good, Dad thought I might like a taste, so he gave me a handful. They were delightfully refreshing.

Dad decided to teach me how to pick my own berries. The only problem is that blackberries grow on brambles, or thorny vines.

But Dad showed me how to find berries low to the ground. Then he showed me how to grab only the big juicy ones and just tug on them.

They come off the vine easy when they are ripe; they're easy pickin'.

Now Dad and I always stop after a long hot hike and treat ourselves to a nice cool refreshing snack of blackberry delights.

We gorge ourselves with so many berries that when we are done, you can tell we've been pickin' 'cause our tongues are stained purple.

Thanksgiving Feast

Fall is the best time of year at the park. It is a time to feast your eyes on colorful foliage and seasoned wildlife.

The main fare is a choice of either wild turkeys gobbling, California quail flushing, or mourning doves cooing.

Side dishes include tree-ripened red apples and oak-grown acorns.

To wash it all down, there is nothing better than ice-cold mountain spring water.

It is all served on a festive table of autumn color including the orange leaves of wild rose briars, yellow and gold oak leaves, and the occasional splash of red willow vines.

To complete the setting, yellow aspen leaves quake and shimmer in the breeze.

What a feast for the senses.

Puzzle

The family was doing a nice puzzle called "Golden Puppies." It was a cute scene of six Golden retriever puppies.

They were putting it together on the dining room table, and I was sitting in one of the chairs at the table, watching them.

I had been studying the puzzle and thought that there was just something missing.

Next morning, I retrieved a shoe and took it with me as I climbed up on the chair. Then it came to me: What the puzzle was missing was a shoe for the puppies to play with.

It looked like the shoe would fit into the puzzle right in the corner, so I dropped it there, and it did fit right into place.

When everyone came out to work on the puzzle, I was still sitting there at the table. They saw that I had dropped the shoe on the puzzle.

They thought that it was hilarious but told me that the shoe wasn't part of the puzzle. They also said that it was sweet of me to be thinking of the puzzle and trying so hard to help them.

I got a big hug too.

"So Help Me Dog"

Dad said I have been watching too much Law and Order on TV.

All because I was sitting on one of the dining room table chairs when someone walked by with their Bible. Thinking I was on the witness stand after having been called to testify, I reached out with one of my paws as they walked by and plopped it right down on that Bible.

I was ready to be sworn in so I could testify.

I was waiting to take the oath: "Do you promise to tell the truth, the whole truth, and nothing but the truth, so help you Dog?"

Dad just broke out in laughter and proclaimed, "Witness excused and case dismissed!"

Canine Express

I communicate with both Mom and Dad, but very differently with each one.

Dad and I communicate intuitively. We are just in sync with each other. We know what each other is thinking, and we just go with it. In so many ways, Dad is like a dog.

Much of our one-on-one time is spent in the great outdoors. Dad uses hand signals to give me direction on the trail. Sometimes, he uses the safety whistle to get my attention and tell me to return to him. Other times, I may balk on the trail when I sense danger or when I want to head back to the ol' black truck.

Indoors, we both know when it's time in the morning for a "butt scratch stomp dance" or in the evening for a before-bed "rough-up."

All this is rather boring in comparison to the communication that me and Mom have. My communication with her is very interactive and stimulating.

We both talk with our paws; we use eye contact and body language. All this in addition to the spoken word and bark.

For instance, when Mom is in the kitchen, we chat it up big time, her in her Mom cave and me on my mat over by the couch. She may comment on a recipe, and I will cock my head or perk up my ears. Perhaps she will say, "This smells amazing," and I will put my twitching nose up in the air and take in all the aroma.

She may invite me to accompany her out into the veggie or herb garden, and of course outside I go, tail wagging all the way.

When it's meal time for me, I sometimes have to remind her. I may have to stare her down or slap my big old paw on her arm. Occasionally, I may bark at her to get her attention. She doesn't like me barking at her and lets me know it too.

When she does start to prepare my meal, I usually do wild spin-arounds in great anticipation of getting fed.

When one of us is sick, the other senses it, and we comfort each other. I may lay down next to her, or she may pet or rub on me.

Mom talks to me in complete sentences, and I understand almost all of it.

Whether it's Mom or Dad, we have great communication with each other.

Bonded

I have an unbreakable bond with both my mom and dad.
Dad and I forged our bond day by day, whereas Mom and I sealed our bond in the midst of a single event.

Most of the pages of this book detail the day-by-day bonding Dad and I experience.

The single event that bonded me and Mom was a terrible thunder and lightning storm.

Mom was napping on the bed. I was getting nervous; something bad was going to happen. Just like that, an explosive clap of thunder followed the crackling lightning bolt that flashed right next to our house.

I thought the world was going to end. Mom jumped up out of her sleep and instantly knew my fear. She tried desperately to get me up on the bed with her, but I was panicked and paralyzed with fear.

Mom wouldn't give up, and in a few minutes I did jump up on the bed with her.

I can't begin to describe the comfort and relief that her warm touch and loving words filled me with.

The storm raged on, but the pounding of my heart and the hyperventilation of my breathing soon began to ease. Mom's arms were like a safe harbor for me.

It wasn't long before I climbed right up on Mom and nearly fell asleep.

That terrible storm finally subsided, but not before the unbreakable bond between me and Mom had been sealed for all time.

Whenever I am scared, I look for Mom, and she always makes it better.

Soul Hearts

Mom and Cookie

Rosemary
Basil
Beans
Peas

There's nothing Mom and I won't plant in the garden. We love to grow our own veggies and herbs.

Then we love to harvest our bounty and cook it up.

In the kitchen, Mom is the chef, and I am her helper and taste-tester. Together, we create delicious five-star meals.

When the world is wild and scary, Mom wraps me in her arms and comforts me.

And when the world is wild and danger lurks, I leap into action to save the day and Mom.

We're gal pals.
We're cuddle buddies.
We're best friends forever.
We share the same heart.
We're soul hearts.

Soul Dogs

Dad and Cookie

Wild winds, hailstorms, blizzards, below-zero temps: Nothing stops me and Dad.

We live to explore our natural world.

We love to discover wild creatures and feast on nature's bounty of beauty.

On the trail, we move as one. I defer to Dad for direction, and he trusts my judgment about danger and our limits.

For the life we live and love so much, we are a perfect match.

We're best buds.

We're pals.

We're partners.

We're two versions of the same spirit and soul.

We're soul dogs.

The Law of the Jungle

Now this is the Law of the Jungle ... as old and true as the sky.

And the Wolf that shall keep it may prosper, but the Wolf that shall break it must die.

As the creeper that girdles the tree-trunk, the Law runneth forward and back—

For the strength of the Pack is the Wolf and the strength of the Wolf is the Pack.

From *The Jungle Book* by Rudyard Kippling

Me and Mom and Dad: We are a pack.

And the strength of our pack is each and all of us.

And the strength of each of us is made more because we are a pack.

Dad says that this law is universal and applies even to our family, and that is why we are a strong and happy pack.

PART THREE

Singing Sand

Dad and I were at Pudding Creek. I was retrieving sticks and running across the beach. As I was scuffling across the sand, we heard a squeaking or whistling noise under my paws.

Dad said that what we were hearing was "singing sand." He said that if the grains of sand are perfectly round, very clean and just a little wet, then the friction of my paws sliding across the sand would cause a compression and shearing effect on the sand and the surrounding air. This effect was what was making the sand sing under my paws.

The sand was singing as Dad walked across the beach too.

The singing of sand occurs in only a few places in the world. It is a very musical sound.

I love to run across the beach at Pudding Creek and make the sand sing.

Sea Glass

Not many dogs can walk across broken glass and even roll around in it, but I do it all the time.

I run across and roll in glass from broken bottles, windshields, and tableware. It doesn't hurt at all. That's cuz Dad takes me to the beach where there is lots of sea glass, which is broken glass that has been tumbled through the sand and surf and rounded into perfect gems of every color imaginable.

So walking on and rolling in broken glass is no big deal and is really fun; it feels so good cuz it scratches you while you are rolling in it.

Soft Serve

Dad always made me nut and 'nilla nogs and they were very yummy.

One day after a long drive transporting dogs to rescue, Dad decided that his deputy dog had earned a nice cool treat, so he stopped and got us both a big serving of soft serve ice cream on our way back home.

Now, whenever we stop for a cool treat, Dad usually gets banana or raspberry or some other special flavor, and he gets me a small cup of frosty vanilla.

Soft serve is very cool and refreshing after a long hot drive. I am able to lick mine without making any mess. I don't even get any on my face or whiskers; I lick the cup completely clean.

Sometimes, I get some of Dad's big cup too.

The Paw Spa

Sometimes, after a long day on her feet at work, Mom comes home and gets a foot massage from Dad. She says that he can take the soreness right out of her feet.

I got to thinking that I walk a lot of miles with Dad when we go on our adventures. I have to scramble over a lot of rough rocks and gravel every day to get to my swimming hole.

When I get home, my feet ache.

So why shouldn't I get a foot massage too?

The very next time Dad gave Mom a foot massage, I got up on the bed as well. When Dad was done with Mom's feet, I just put one of my paws right into his hand. Mom laughed and said, "Cookie wants you to rub her feet too."

Dad grabbed my foot and rubbed each and every pad. Then he took the other foot and rubbed it too. He massaged all four of my feet. When he finished, he had taken the soreness right out of my feet, just like Mom said.

When I got down from the bed, I was walking on air.

Whenever me and Mom have sore feet, we just make an appointment with Dad at the Paw Spa.

Beaver-Splash Dance

Tails were slapping, and water was raining down. It was wet and wild. I was awash in a splash dance.

That's what Dad said about the day me and three beavers went dancing in the lake.

It all started when the beavers swam around the point where we were standing. They saw us, slapped their tails on the surface, and then disappeared underwater.

Shortly, one of the beavers popped up, and we were eye-to-eye. I couldn't resist the temptation, and in the water I went. And so the dance began.

For thirty minutes, I chased those beavers, catching up to one, only to have it smack its tail again and completely drench me in a shower of water. Then underwater it went again.

So off I swam after another partner; on and on I danced with those beavers. Farther and farther out onto the watery dance floor we went. Halfway across the lake we danced, them splashing me and me chasing them.

It must have been quite entertaining for Dad as he stood there on the shore watching our performance.

Finally, after half an hour, Dad called me back to shore, and the beavers went gliding back to their lodge.

It was a dance like no other: a real splash dance.

River Otter– Super Slide

One day, Dad and I were hiking quietly down a trail at the park. We could hear purring and growling sounds coming from two lily ponds along the trail.

We froze motionless and soon saw a River Otter emerging from the smaller of the two ponds. It ran up a mud bank and then slid back down the other side into the bigger pond.

A second otter then ran up the mud slide and pushed itself off with its front feet tucked tightly to its side. It quickly gained momentum as it sped down the slick mud bank and plunged into the smaller pond. It purred all the way down into the pond; we could then hear it growling underwater.

Unaware of their audience, back and forth these two river otters joyfully played. They took turns super sliding and splashing into one pond and then the other.

Dad said that sliding is a favorite playtime activity for river otters. They were certainly having as much fun as any kid at a waterpark or any kid running through a backyard sprinkler.

Porcupine

Earlier this spring, Mom, Dad and I came across a very prickly creature waddling along the edge of an alder grove. He was lazily grazing on the grass and clover.

I approached very carefully because he was the oddest thing I had ever seen. He had a spiked haircut and was clad in a heavy coat of black and white quills. As we approached, he arched his back and retreated slowly back into the woods.

He was very well fed and kind of porky. Dad said what we saw was a Porcupine. He said they strip the bark off trees and eat other vegetation as well. They can be considered as pests in some situations. They can often be seen resting up on tree limbs. Dad said we should give him lots of room because with just one swipe of his spiny tail, we could become stuck with hundreds of his barbed quills.

We saw ol' Porky Pine again a few days after that; we enjoyed watching him at the edge of the woods. After that, we never saw him again.

Turtle

On our way to Dead Lake, Dad would sometimes pull the truck over, get out and move rocks off the road. I never understood why he didn't just drive around them.

Then one day, we were walking along a trail next to a big lily pond. I saw one of those rocks right in the middle of the trail. As we got closer, I couldn't believe what I saw. The rock started walking down the trail!

I ran up to the rock and its head and legs disappeared. I sniffed it, barked at it and even scratched it with my paw, but it would not move.

Dad told me that the rock was really a Western Pond Turtle and that she was looking for a safe place, away from the pond, to lay her eggs.

On our way down the trail, we turned and watched the turtle scamper away to safety.

Turtles are a lot like rocks.

Hounds 1

There was a dog hoarding and neglect incident reported to the animal control shelter. Dad and his staff had to take in over twenty dogs.

Among the dogs taken in were five Bloodhounds. They were underweight, weak and had badly irritated and infested ears that were quite smelly.

Mom administered the vet prescribed treatment medicine. She squeezed the recommended dose of drops into the hounds ears and rubbed and massaged them so that the meds were worked deep into their ears. This brought instant relief to the hounds and they loved it.

Finally, Mom twisted up a paper towel and worked it down the hounds ear canals.

This captured and removed any dead mites. Soon they quit shaking their heads and scratching at their ears.

After that, Mom was their best friend.

The hounds faces and necks were very wrinkly and their long soft ears hung low in graceful folds.

Aside from their neglected condition, the Bloodhounds were very friendly and loveable; they wagged their tails constantly.

Hounds 2

The Bloodhounds soon recovered from their infestation of ear mites and regained a normal body weight. They were all happy and healthy and very affectionate towards staff and the public.

What really won the hearts of me and Mom and Dad though was their howling.

We lived in a small trailer next to the dog kennels that we affectionately called Kennel #33.

Nearly every night, the Bloodhounds serenaded us with the most beautiful and melodious song. One hound would throw its head back and begin a deep and prolonged baying sound. Then, one by one, the other hounds chimmed in with perfect harmony. They became a quintet of howling hounds. Many nights we were lulled to sleep by their wonderful vocalizations. We looked forward to and loved hearing their harmonious lullibies.

Eventually, Dad sent all the Bloodhounds to a hound rescue that could place them with families who could meet the special needs of their breed.

Woody 1

Woody was a pound dog who presented a puzzle to everyone when it came to determining his breed. He looked like a Labrador retriever, yet he was reddish in color. The local Humane Society was puzzled by Woody too.

Dad and I eventually transported Woody to a rescue organization in Oregon. When we got there, the rescue staff asked Dad if he knew what he had in Woody.

Dad explained that the shelter was confused about what Woody's breed was.

The rescue told Dad that Woody was a fox red Labrador retriever. This was a total surprise to Dad. Apparently, fox red is a recognized color for Labradors; it is a dark phase of a yellow Lab.

So as it turns out, Labradors come in four colors: black, chocolate, yellow, and fox red; who knew?

Woody 2

Soon after Woody went to the Oregon rescue, he had to be returned to Dad's shelter. The rescue said that Woody was suffering from separation anxiety. He really missed Dad.

I went with Dad again to go pick up Woody and bring him back home.

We felt sorry for Woody, so we stopped along the river on our way back and went swimming.

Unfortunately, Woody had never been swimming. I decided I would teach him how to swim.

Dad threw a stick in the water a few times, and I retrieved it and brought it back to Dad. Woody was very interested and seemed to be processing what he was seeing.

Then Dad threw two sticks into the water. I swam out to retrieve one of the sticks, and just like that, Woody went in too. He was very clumsy in the water, splashing wildly with his front paws as he tried to paddle out to the other stick. He barely stayed afloat as he reached the stick and grabbed it in his mouth. He did make it back to shore, splashing all the way.

By the time we were ready to load up and get back on the road, we could barely get Woody out of the water. He had swimming dialed in and no longer splashed as he swam. He moved smoothly through the water, with his feet underwater and his chin resting on the surface.

I had taught Woody how to swim.

Dad took him to Dead Lake frequently so he could swim and retrieve.

Woody soon grew more confident about himself and became more independent.

Eventually, Woody was adopted into a great home.

Spud

Spud harnessed to his wheel cart

Spud was a snow-white Pit Bull. His story is both tragic and inspirational.

Spud was picked up as a stray and impounded into the animal control shelter. In a few days, he was redeemed back to his owner, who then entrusted Spud to a friend of his.

Unfortunately, Spud ran astray again, and the very next day, he was hit by a car. He was seriously injured when law enforcement brought him back to the shelter.

Spud was taken to the vet for examination. The vet told Dad that Spud had a severed spine and would never be able to walk again. He said he could undertake a very expensive surgery to try to give Spud some mobility, but he also said his quality of life would be greatly reduced. Neither the shelter staff nor the local Humane Society held any hope for Spud.

But my dad never gave up hope. He found someone in New York City who was willing to donate money for the surgery. Spud had his surgery and gained some additional mobility but was unable to stand and walk.

Meanwhile, Dad also put out an internet plea for help for Spud. In no time, a rescue sanctuary in Montana answered the plea and said they would take him.

Dad gave Spud lots of attention and encouragement, and it didn't take long for Spud to imprint onto Dad.

Soon Dad arranged a transport shuttle to get Spud up to Montana. Dad drove the first leg of the transport, and Spud laid in his lap the whole way.

It was a tearful goodbye when Dad handed Spud off to the next driver. Dad gave Spud one of his old shirts, stinky with his scent, to take with him on his transport and to keep with him at the sanctuary.

A year later, the staff at the Montana sanctuary had renamed Spud, Mr. Spud Sparkles. He was running along the river in a custom-made wheel cart. Staff could not keep up with him on his walks. In winter, his wheel cart was fitted with skis, and Spud became quite a skier.

Spud was so positive and happy that the sanctuary made him an ambassador dog. He visited schools, hospitals, and other animal rescues. He became quite the inspiration for all handicapped creatures, two- and four-leggeds alike.

Dad and I are very happy for Spud. His life began tragically, but because of his positive attitude, he has become an inspiration to all.

Roland, the Tail-Waggin' Dog

Roland was a dog who got in the way of a moving car and was severely injured.

Dad and I were out of town when the call came from Dad's office about Roland. Dad said he should be taken to the vet's office for examination.

Instead of putting Roland down, the vet placed him on meds and said that if someone made an effort to get him on his feet and walk him, he might recover from his injuries and be rehabilitated.

Dad worked with Roland often. He was a very sweet and happy dog, brindle in marking, who loved to wag his tail and lay in the grass.

Sadly, after two weeks, Roland passed away. There must have been internal damage as well.

On his last morning, Dad laid Roland on the lawn atop a nice thick purple comforter. Dad petted him every few minutes. I saw Roland laying there and knew he was very sick. I had never witnessed a dog pass away before.

Roland passed away, laying in the cool, shaded grass he loved so much, and he wagged his tail for Dad right to the very end.

Dad says there is much man and dog can learn from Roland.

He was a good dog, and we see him running the Milky Way whenever we look up into the night sky.

RIP, ol' friend.

Just a Slice

Dad jokes and says, "Save a slice for me."

What he means is that I sleep on the bed and usually take my half right down the middle of the bed.

So poor old Dad has to take a slice of the bed wherever he can find it. He seems to be ok with it, though; I always leave the last little slice of the pie for him. It's usually right on the very edge of the bed too.

Cloud 9

I'm on Cloud 9, a billowy, fluffy, and comfy mound of cumulous clouds floating across the sky.

It's so soft and comfortable. It brings me happiness and such a blissful sleep.

I'm on Cloud 9, twelve inches of memory foam atop Mom and Dad's bed.

It fits and forms to my body and takes away all of my aches and pains. I sleep hard all night and wake up revived and refreshed, ready for the day's adventure.

Yep, I am on Cloud 9.

Swimming in my Dreams

Mom and Dad tell me that when I'm asleep at night, I dream about swimming. They say that because I always twitch my feet in my sleep.

You know what? They're right.

When I'm sleeping, I might dream about swimming alongside Dad in the canoe. He always slows down so I can keep up with him. Many times, I wind up swimming all the way across the lake. Then, I might get on the canoe and ride back, or I might just want to swim all the way back alongside the canoe.

Sometimes, I dream about Dad throwing sticks into the water for me to retrieve. In my dreams, I retrieve sticks for Dad nonstop, for hours.

Other times, I dream about having fun with beavers. I love it when they slap their tails atop the water, dive down, and then resurface behind me. I have to turn in the water and chase after them in a new direction. On and on we go like this, just having fun with each other.

Almost every night, on the bed, Mom and Dad can feel me twitching my feet wildly, and they say one to the other, "Cookie's dreaming about swimming again."

No doubt about it; I live, breathe, and dream about swimming. It's my passion.

Scarecrow

Me and my Mom and Dad toured a botanical garden along the coast. There was a dahlia garden, pumpkin patch and lots of other beautiful displays.

Mom was walking me on my leash. We were viewing one of the displays when I looked up and nearly jumped out of my fur. The hair on my back stood up and I began barking and snarling.

Standing atop a hay bale, staring down at me, was a menacing figure that looked to be at least ten feet tall. Straw was poking out of its overalls and hat. Mom tried to calm me down. She reached out and rubbed its arm to show me that everything was ok. Cautiously, I sniffed at it and started to settle down.

When I finally relaxed, Mom and Dad explained to me that the figure was just a garden scarecrow stuffed with lots of straw. Its job was to scare off garden pests like birds and rodents.

All I can say is that scarecrow scared the heck out of me!

Sea Creature

Walking on a California beach, I watched a strange creature emerge out of the surf. It was completely black, walked on two legs and carried a big piece of driftwood.

The creature started walking down the beach. I was curious but hesitant. With my tail between my legs, I began to follow from a safe distance. Finally, Mom and Dad whistled me back.

They explained to me that the creature I was following was just a surfer in a hooded wet suit, with booties, carrying his surfboard. They pointed to other surfers in the ocean.

That satisfied my curiosity and relieved my anxiety. I thought that I had seen some new, undiscovered sea creature.

Bumble Bee

Bumble bees on Fuller's Teasels

It has been a very good year for bumble bees. Dad says that lots of bumble bees are a good sign that our local environment is healthy and diverse. Bumble bees forage for nectar and pollinate wild plants like clover and mint and also ornamental plants like fuchsias.

They are really big bees colored in yellow and black. They make their nests in the ground. They are very cute creatures, and it is a lot of fun to watch them buzzing around from plant to plant as they collect nectar and pollen.

Dad says that bumble bees are very gentle creatures, but they have barbless stingers. If we were to disturb or harm them, they could sting us multiple times. Dad loves them, though, and even lets them crawl over his hands as he holds them. He says he has never been stung by a bumble bee.

    Bumble bees are one of Dad's favorite creatures, but I stay clear of them because I wouldn't want them to get caught in my fur. If they did, I'm sure I'd get stung as I tried to get them off me with my paws.

Ant

All year, we have been observing two big ant hills at Dead Lake. They are the home of some pretty aggressive red and black ants called Western Thatch Ants.

I first noticed them early in the spring. I saw some movement on top of a big dirt pile littered with bits of grass and plant material. Being curious, I was attracted to the movement of the ants on the top of the hill. As I approached, I pawed at the little creatures scampering all about. That was a mistake, as it didn't take long for those little critters to bite the heck out of my foot. It hurt like crazy, and I had a sore foot for a few days afterwards; they packed quite a wallop.

Later in the summer, a bear came and dug out both ant hills, eating the baby ant grubs. One of the colonies was completely killed out, but the other one survived, and in time, it was completely rebuilt and repopulated. The queen ant in that colony must have survived the marauding bear.

Today, that colony is as big and busy as ever, standing almost two feet in height.

I learned to leave ants alone, 'cause there is fire in the hole.

Tick

I hate it when Dad messes with me, like when he checks how long my nails are or when he puts stuff on me for fleas.

But worst of all is when he has to pull ticks off me. I am always running through the brush, so I'm going to pick up ticks from time to time.

They are nasty; they seem to always latch onto me in or around my ears or on my forehead near my eyes or even on my chest.

It's hard for Dad to get them off of me. He has to grab them just right and then twist them a quarter turn to the left before he yanks them off of me. Most of the time, he also pulls off some fur along with the ticks.

I just hate going through all of this. Sometimes, I am not too cooperative, and I snarl and show my teeth to Dad, but he says it's important to keep me tick free so I don't get sick.

Daughter

Cookie: She's our daughter.
    She was eight weeks old when I bought her.
    From the very start I taught her
all about the water.
Cookie: She's like an otter.
She's retrieved all the sticks I got her.
Each and every day, I've caught her
always in the water.
Cookie: She's our otter daughter.

Ma's Home

"Ma's home; Ma's home; Cookie, Ma's home," Dad says. Whenever I hear Mom drive in after work or after she has run her errands, I am very excited to see her. My tail starts wagging wildly, and I do spin-arounds. Even if she has been gone for only five minutes, I am so happy she is home.

Mom always gives me a scoobie treat when she gets home, and she always talks to me, letting me know that she missed me too.

I sure love my mom; she is the greatest.

Ma's Paws

My paws are very important; they get me where I am going, on land and in the water.

I need to keep them clean and well-groomed every day. When I get back home from my adventure with Dad, I get up on the couch and work on every paw, removing stickers, gravel, and splinters from between my pads and from under my nails.

Just as important as my paws are, so are Ma's paws. She keeps her nails painted pretty and sexy, so it is necessary for me to lick them clean every morning and every night at bedtime.

As crazy as it sounds, every once in a while, I even lick Pa's big ol' rough paws too.

My paws, Ma's paws, and Pa's paws.

The Butt Scratch Stomp Dance

After a night of hard sleeping, I wake up in the morning happy to see Dad and really fired up.

The first thing we do is head for the dance floor in the living room in front of the recliner.

I start off ramming and rubbing against the couch and recliner. Then Dad roughs me up by scratching my butt.

Back and forth I go under Dad's arms as he scratches me. It feels great, and I throw my head back, flick my tongue out, and stomp my back feet.

There's nothing that gets your morning off to a better start than doing the Butt Scratch Stomp Dance.

River Otter-Fillet-O-Bass

Dad and I were at one of the secluded coves at Dead Lake one winter day.

While standing there taking in the sights, sounds, and smells, I heard a rustling in the grass along the shoreline. As I stepped along the fallen log to investigate, a River Otter, his face full of fish, dove into the water and swam off.

When I got over to where the otter had been hidden in the grass, I saw what remained of a big, half-eaten bass.

Dad said that during winter the water is a lot colder than in summer, and the fish in the lake move much slower. He said this is what allowed the otter to catch such a big fish.

He said that after we were gone, the river otter would probably return and finish his tasty meal of fillet-o-bass.

Pheasant Flushing

Trotting down the trail, I caught the scent of something in the bush. I froze in position with my paw held up, my tail outstretched, and my muzzle aimed right where I thought there was something hidden.

I wanted Dad to see where it was, so I held my position.

After a few seconds, the brush exploded in a flurry of thrashing wings. I had just flushed out a Ring-necked Pheasant.

She wasn't the only one, either. After the first one took off, I worked the field and found six more. I flushed them out too, one at a time.

They all flew off to the other end of the field and landed in the safety of the brush there.

It all happened in less than a minute. It was very exciting to see all those pheasants flushing out in such a frenzy.

Ducklings

Dad and I were walking down the trail at Dead Lake late one day this spring. The trail was grown over, and the ponds were full.

As we were walking down the trail, a female Mallard duck, who must have been in the water near the trail, lifted off and flew away.

I continued walking down the trail with my retrieving stick in my mouth. The next thing I knew, I was being overtaken by thirteen bright yellow ducklings.

They were running down the trail after their mamma and were quacking loudly. They were scampering between my legs and all around me. I was in a sea of fluffy yellow down.

Finally, the ducklings got past me and kept running, single file, down the trail.

It wasn't long before they darted off the trail and into another pond, where they were once again reunited with their mamma.

It all happened so fast and was very chaotic.

Grandma's Goodies

I love going to visit Grandma. She's Ma's Ma.

When we go to Grandma's house, I like to sit in the kitchen doorway and watch her cook. Grandma's cooking smells great, just like Ma's does.

Sooner or later though, I can't resist the temptation of the goodies that Grandma puts on her coffee table for us to snack on.

There's lots of cookies and candy and nuts.

I'm so clever and handy. When nobody is looking, I can unwrap a piece of candy as slick as you please and gobble it down.

I leave the wrapper right there on the coffee table next to the candy dish. There's never any teeth marks or slobber left behind and nobody is the wiser that it was me who got into the candy.

I love Grandma's goodies!

Barrel of Barks

Dad says that life with me is not exactly a barrel of laughs, nor is it a barrel of monkeys, either. Life with me, he says, is a barrel of barks.

He says I have a bark for every occasion. He says that barking is one of the ways I communicate.

I bark differently when I express curiosity, playfulness, impatience, protection, fear, anger, aggression, and dominance, among other feelings.

All of my barks can vary in number, loudness, tone, and intensity; sometimes, I also growl when I bark.

Mom has taught me to use what she calls an "inside bark." It is like a bark with a silencer. She has me use this inside bark so she and Dad can hear the TV or radio or when they are trying to sleep.

Mom has to remind me to use my inside bark most of the time. Sometimes, I slip and go back to my loud barking anyway, and other times, I just don't listen and don't use my inside bark at all.

Camo

My black coat is the perfect suit of camouflage.
No matter where I am, I am hard to see. At a distance, I look like I'm in the shadows. I am totally undetectable. In the grass, in the brush, or in the trees, I can't be seen.

At night, I disappear into darkness. Mom and Dad don't even see me when I'm at their feet. I can't even be seen when I move in the dark.

My black coat is the perfect suit of camouflage, except in winter. Then, I am a black peppercorn on a blanket of snowflakes. I can be seen for miles; I am impossible to miss; I stick out like a sore thumb.

Well, my coat is almost perfect.

Multitasking

Dad says I am good at multitasking.

The other day, I was trotting down the trail with my retrieving stick in my mouth when I saw some movement in the grass. It's just instinct for me to stop, lift my foot, straighten my tail, and point at whatever critter is rattling around in the brush.

Dad laughs and says it's quite a sight to see me pointing with my stick in my mouth.

Other times, I pack my stick, point, then go to digging out rodents.

He says it gives new meaning to the phrase "multitasking." It's nothing new to me, though; I can do lots of things at the same time.

Bio Clock

Our home has three tall windows that stretch from ceiling to floor. This makes my job of guarding the house and protecting Mom and Dad so easy that I can actually lay down while on duty.

We live in a senior park, so our neighbors follow a strict daily routine. They and their dogs walk the same route at the same time every day.

I come to attention before Mom and Dad even see the walkers. They think this is very impressive; but it is just my biological clock telling me that soon one of our neighbors will be coming into view and passing our house.

This is the same clock that tells me Dad will soon be home for lunch or home for the day after work. It's the same clock that tells me when it's time to eat, time to go on an adventure, or time for whatever I set it for.

Stiff Neck

It's always been the bigger the stick, the better for me to retrieve.

Well, Dad found one that was so big and heavy that every time he threw it into the river for me to retrieve, he nearly pulled a muscle. That stick was more like a big ol' log.

That log was so big and heavy that I could barely get my mouth around it. I had to swing my tail in the water, like a ship's rudder, just to get myself turned around and headed back to shore.

To top it off, the entry into the river was a steep drop-off, with no chance for me to walk out of the water; I had to climb out of the river with the log in my mouth. On the third retrieve, I felt something pull in my neck as I was climbing up and out of the river.

The next morning, I was in pain and couldn't even get out of bed. Mom slid the mattress over and then tipped it so I could slide down to the floor. She gave me low-dose, safety-coated aspirin all day and the next day too. That helped with the pain, but I was really immobile.

It took a week of meds and rest for me to heal up and regain my mobility enough to take walks with Dad again.

Dad said, "It's short, light beaver sticks for retrieving, and no swimming in places with steep drop-offs. Only low-impact retrieving for Cookie from now on."

After that painful, crippling stiff neck, they won't get any arguments from me. No more macho-dog power swimming anymore; I'm getting a little too old for that. Good ol' low-impact retrieving is just fine with me from now on.

Slowing Down

Dad says I am slowing down some. It's no wonder; Dad says he figures I have swum at least a thousand times. He says we have hiked close to ten thousand miles together.

He says he sees me laboring some when I go to jump onto the bed or into the truck. So he's been having me step onto a folding chair when I have to jump up. Also, we have cut back a little on how far we walk every day. We still swim almost every day, though.

Mom and Dad are going to start giving me bone and joint supplements so that I don't break down in the hips or get arthritis. They want me to be pain free for a long time. We have a lot of adventures ahead of us yet in the coming years.

Feeling Better

I've been taking those hip and joint supplements I told you about for a few months now.

Wow ... they have really kicked in.

I'm walking with a real spring in my step again. I have lots of energy on my walks, and I even take off sprinting across the sand dunes again, like I used to do.

My body has been restored, and I am pretty much pain free.

Dad still keeps me out of the water when it is really cold outside, and I have scaled down the lengths of my walks. I still step onto a chair when getting on the bed or into the cars and truck.

Mom and Dad are sure great doctors.

I feel like I could live forever.

Beaver-Bone of our Bones

The beaver fells the trees
   that slow the water
   that fills the pond
where I swim.
The beaver cuts the sticks
that Dad throws
that I retrieve in the pond
that the beaver builds.
The beaver stocks his pond
with frogs and fish
that Dad catches
and I chase in the pond
that the beaver builds.
When winter comes
the beaver snuggles cozy
in a lodge of logs
while Dad and I skate the frozen pond
that the beaver builds
by felling trees
that slow the water
that fills the pond
where I swim
and retrieve sticks
that the beaver cuts

that Dad throws into the pond
that the beaver stocks
with frogs and fish
that Dad catches and I chase
in the pond
that the beaver builds.
Bone of our bones,
we are one:
beavers and retrievers
and Dad too!

Bear

Bear carving

Dad and I were on our morning walk at the shelter recently. As we looked down the lane that leads to the airport, we saw a huge black dog at the end of the trail. As we looked more closely, we realized it was a Black Bear. As I ran down to investigate, it quickly disappeared into the brush.

The bear has become a regular visitor at the shelter grounds. He comes at night and really raises Cain with the dogs; they bark and go wild when they see or smell him. The bear leaves his muddy paw prints all over the livestock trailer and barn doors; he also leaves big piles of bear poop. He crawls into the barn and makes a huge mess as he rummages through the grain sacks, gorging himself and scattering the rest of the grain and bags everywhere.

He has become a real nuisance in the general area, tearing down all kinds of fences, swiping his sharp paws at dogs and other animals and injuring them. He causes a lot of property damage.

We try to keep the barn area secure and bear-proof, but he still comes around in the middle of the night. Sometimes, Dad fires a rifle into the air to run the bear off; that usually works.

Dad cautioned me to stay clear of this smelly and grumpy critter, and I do. I don't want to get shredded by those razor-sharp claws.

R-Pod

Mom and Dad got a new travel trailer recently. It's a cute little eighteen-foot teardrop called an R-Pod.

It's equipped with a cozy warm furnace and a really cool air conditioner, so sleeping on the four-inch memory foam pad on the bunk is heavenly.

There's decals of frogs fishing on lily pads on the sides. Dad even added a few of his own, like a couple of beaver decals and a couple of big black Labrador retriever decals.

We all love camping in the R-Pod. Dad says I seem to love it so much that R-Pod stands for Retriever-Pod.

The Jolly Black Giant

Next to berries, the best parts of the veggie garden are the green beans and peas.

Watching Mom pick the beans and peas, it didn't take me long to figure out how to pick my own. All I have to do is grab 'em and pull 'em off the vine. It's just like picking blackberries. And there's no reason to bring 'em in and cook 'em up; they're sweet and yummy right off the vine.

I love going out to the garden with Mom to harvest the veggies; she picks a handful or so of beans and peas for me.

Dad even says I watch over our garden just like the Green Giant does; he actually calls me the Jolly Black Giant.

Ma's Sauce

A dog's nose is many times more sensitive than that of a two-legged.

For example, if Dad says he smells lasagna cooking in the oven, I say I smell the spicy sausage, I smell the garlic, I smell the onions, I smell the basil, and I smell the tomatoes.

Dad smells lasagna, but I smell each and every ingredient in the lasagna.

Mom is a good ol' Italian girl who grew up in the kitchen, cooking with her ma and grandma. So when she combines fresh basil, oregano, garlic, tomatoes, and onions into her homemade sauce, my nose starts twitching, and my tastebuds dance with mouthwatering delight.

The anticipation of a spoonful of that savory Italian sauce on my nightly ration of hard kibble drives me wild. When she serves up my dinner, I beat her to the feed stand. I don't even come up for air until I have licked up every last taste of her famous sauce. My bowl is so shiny, you can see yourself in it.

Raccoon Bandits

Dad and I got bushwhacked by a gang of masked marauders down at the beach recently. They all wore black facemasks and stripes.

We were combing the beach at dusk when all of a sudden, a rock outcrop boiled over with loud hissing and the sound of gnashing teeth. There were as many as half a dozen bandits that charged me and Dad.

It was every dog for itself, so I took off running for safety as fast as I could, until the bandit after me broke off from its chase.

Meanwhile, I looked back at Dad and saw that he had taken up high ground and was wildly waving his arms and yelling loudly. Finally, all of the crazed Raccoons took off for parts unknown, leaving us breathing a big sigh of relief.

After a while, when all was clear and safe, I rejoined Dad. He said we had run onto a group of 'coons who had been feasting on a bounty of shellfish exposed by the minus tide. Apparently, we had posed some sort of threat to them, and they charged us aggressively in an effort to protect their treasure.

We were lucky, as they really meant business and could have been rabid. Next time, we won't go beachcombing so late in the day, and we'll be sure to bring along a nice big walking stick, just in case.

Elephant Seals

Me and Mom and Dad were beachcombing and picking sea glass along the coast late one spring afternoon.

Mom spotted some female Elephant Seals, maybe twenty of them, basking on the rocks at the edge of the tide.

They held my attention captive the entire time we were at the beach. They were really big and a beautiful shade of tan.

Dad said it was the start of the molting season. By the time July rolls around, they will have lost a lot of fur and skin, and they will be ready to head to sea to feed on fish and other marine life. Then when the mating season begins next January, they will once again come ashore for breeding and birthing.

The seals remained basking on the rocks the entire time we were at the beach.

Handicapped

I need a handicap placard. Dad could keep it in his truck when we go on our adventures. Also, Mom could take it with her when she drives with me in her ruby-red Jeep.

It's hard for me to move now; I'm not as flexible or mobile as I used to be. I need as much assistance as I can get nowadays.

That's why I climb into vehicles by stepping onto a folding chair first, then when I get out, I walk down my sliding ramp.

The same applies for me when I am getting onto and off of our bed.

It's hard getting older, and no fun, either.

Bittersweet

Today is a big day for me and Dad.
    Today we are both 22,536 days old. Seniors both, to be sure.

We have been together all of my nine years, and it has been a great life of adventure and fun.

In all that time, I have been Dad's baby.

Come tomorrow, our world will be upside down. I will become older than Dad.

Time marches on, only it marches on faster for me.

Every day, every adventure is even more precious now.

Bittersweet.

The Milky Way

One night, Dad and I sat atop Diamond Mountain, peering into the starry sky with a sense of wonder.

I asked Dad about the big white cloud of stars in the sky, so he told me Native legends about the Milky Way.

Dad said legend tells of Native people who pounded corn flour every night. Then one morning, they found that some was missing.

The next night, they watched and saw a dog come from the north and eat some of their white flour. The people chased the dog, but he ran back north and up into the sky. As the dog ran, he left a white trail called "where the dog ran" or "the dog way," or as we know it, the Milky Way.

Dad said it is legend that the dog way is a sky path for the souls and spirits of dogs and other animals.

As we sat atop the mountain, gazing into the midnight sky, Dad put his arm around me. At once, we were at peace in the knowledge that one day I too will be running the dog way and that all Dad has to do to see me is to look up into the night sky at the Milky Way.

I will always be there, waiting to see Dad.

PART FOUR

Deer

2 Bucks

Sometimes, the cost of fun can be really cheap, like just two bucks.

That's the kind of fun Dad and I had a few days ago.

We were walking along the river when a small herd of White-tailed Deer scampered out of the brush, right in front of us.

We froze motionless, and the herd stopped just a few feet in front of us and began grazing on meadow grass. They seemed oblivious to us.

Dad slowly got his camera out and focused on the two forked-horned bucks standing side by side. They shifted position, still side by side, with one in front of the other, and they just gazed straight at us. Dad snapped a pic of them in this classic pose, with their velvet antlers silhouetted against a background of green brush and grass.

That pic now hangs in our man/dog cave to remind us that the best fun doesn't even cost two bucks; it's free.

Mink

When I think of some of the great adventures that Dad and I have had, I think Mink.

Like the time we were down at the river and I was retrieving sticks in the water.

Just then, we heard a commotion by the rocks along the shore. Dad and I looked up and saw two dark-brown furry creatures playing peek-a-boo with us. They would poke their heads up to see us and just as quickly duck back down. After doing this several times, they would playfully chase after each other across the rocks.

After a while, they ran into the water and swam around in front of us for a minute or so before disappearing upriver.

I had never seen creatures like this before. Dad said we had just seen two mink.

Sea Otter-Beachcombing

Dad and I were walking a remote ocean beach on a very stormy day at minus tide.

Up ahead, we saw what looked like a dog running on the beach. As we got closer, we realized what we were really seeing was a Sea Otter.

We watched that otter scamper over to a big rock covered with lots of California Mussels. The otter stood on its back flippers and began prying and twisting large mussels off the rock. Then it smashed them against the rock and skillfully used its front feet to open the shells and began feasting on its fresh bounty.

The otter soon spotted us and headed back into the ocean surf, so Dad and I went over to the big rock and saw lots of broken mussel shells.

Dad said we had just witnessed a rarely seen behavior. He said it just went to prove how clever and resourceful otters really are.

Grouse

One of the first places Dad and I explored after we moved to Oregon was a small secluded pond on Ferry Creek that was not far from town.

That day, as we hiked through the woods on our way to the pond, we neared a thicket of brush and alder. Then, just as I caught scent of something, a pile of dead leaves at the base of the alder trees exploded in a flash of mottled wings.

We jumped out of our skin, and our hearts were pounding as two chicken-like birds with rounded bodies and gray tail bands burst straight up and out of the leaves, then darted deeper into the woods.

Dad said we had just flushed out two Ruffed Grouse.

It was an exciting and thrilling few seconds that I will never forget.

Heron and Egret

Almost every dinner table is set with salt and pepper shakers; side by side they sit atop the table.

Every fall, the lake recedes and allows us to walk along exposed shorelines and explore areas we haven't been able to access all year.

Just the other day, Dad and I were able to reach the north end of Dead Lake, where there were lots of pond lilies and fallen logs.

As we rounded a bend, we were rewarded with an amazing sight. Sitting side by side on an old log were a dark Great Blue Heron and a Snowy Egret. Together, they sat just like a pair of salt and pepper shakers on a table.

After a few minutes, they both flew off on their separate ways.

We will always remember this especially well-seasoned sighting.

Freedom

Freedom is important to me. Dad gives me freedom when he lets me run loose and untethered when we go on our adventures.

This allows me to explore the great outdoors using all of my canine senses: sight, sound, smell, taste, and touch.

Because of this freedom, I have become the dog that God made me to be.

Let freedom ring!

Responsibility

Just as important as freedom is to me, so too is responsibility.

My responsibility is to take care of and protect Mom and Dad and to guard our home and property.

It is the most important job a dog can have.

Fulfilling my responsibility gives purpose to my life and makes me want to get up every day.

My Ol' Black Truck

Cookie's ol' black truck

I love my ol' black truck; it's the only truck I've ever had.

It has no power steering, no power brakes, and no electric windows. My truck hasn't been tuned up in seven years; it's old, rusty, and sweaty.

I have the inside of the windows in my ol' black truck smeared with my nose prints.

I love my truck because when Dad starts it up, it means that he and I are going to go have an adventure or maybe I will just be going to tag along with Dad as he does his errands.

When I am riding in my truck, I get to lay across Dad's lap and gnaw on my knuckle bone.

When we get back to the truck after our adventure, I jump back in and there's always a scoobie treat laying there on the seat for me.

On our way home, Dad rolls down the windows so I can get lots of fresh air blowing in my face.

I sure do love my ol' black truck.

Honk Dog

After over a quarter-century, my ol' black truck has a few things that don't exactly work right.

The thing that drives Dad crazy the most is the truck's horn. He hasn't been able to get it to honk for at least a couple of years.

But all I have to do is bump it with my snout, and it honks every time. I have the magic touch.

Dad even tries pushing on the horn exactly where I do and right after I do, but he can never get that horn to honk.

He just throws up his hands in frustration and says, "Cookie, you're just a big honking dog."

Peanut Butter Scoobies

One of the few joys of growing older is getting spoiled, especially being spoiled with extra treats.

Whenever Dad takes me on an adventure, he gives me a hard biscuit when we get back to the truck. I call these treats "scoobies."

Mom gives me a scoobie first thing in the morning and first thing when she comes home from work or from errands.

Best of all though are the treats I get in the morning and at bedtime. These scoobies have peanut butter smeared on them. My bone and joint supplements are put into the peanut butter, and I gobble them down in no time.

I always get a fresh pot of cool, clean water so I can wash my treats down.

I love peanut butter.

Stop and Smell the Roses

They say you should slow down, stop, and smell the roses and just enjoy life.
    Well, I do love and enjoy my life, but I like to stop and smell the herbs.

Yes, that's right. I love the smell of my mom's herb garden: basil, rosemary, cilantro, lavender, tarragon, and dill. Wow, what a delight the herb garden is.

Dogs have great noses, and Mom's herbs give my nose a real workout.

Mountain Lion

There have been a few times when I have balked and refused to continue on the trail because I sensed great danger.

This was especially true on our hikes into Cottonwood Grove. That trail was flanked with high rimrocked ridges on both sides. That is perfect habitat for Mountain Lions; they can hang out on the ridges and see everything down below. Occasionally, I knew we were being watched, so I alerted Dad by balking.

Dad always trusted my instinct and judgment and never led us further into danger; we always retreated back to safety.

Dad said it is far better to be cautious than reckless and far better to be safe than fall prey to such a formidable predator. After all, it was the mountain lion's world we were adventuring into.

Turkey

One day, Dad and I were walking along the river when my nose was filled with the scent of something wild. I worked that scent all along the river, tracking back and forth.

Finally, in the grass near some alder trees, I locked in and looked up, catching sight of two dark-colored birds. I no sooner pointed them than they sprang into flight. They were two big plump birds.

Dad laughed and said I had just served up a couple of big butterballs: two wild Turkeys.

Strangely, they flew a short distance and then landed in the branches of a tree at the edge of the river. We walked toward the tree and watched them for a few minutes before we went on our way.

Crickets

Early one morning, Dad and I awoke at home to a symphony of sounds and activity.

In the wetlands, frogs were croaking and crickets were chirping.

Across the dawning sky, migrating geese cackled as they flew in formation.

A pair of hooting owls serenaded us from atop a big cottonwood tree.

It was an amazing experience. It was a social gathering; it was a celebration of singing and dancing.

It was a real hootenanny.

Cooking It Up

Ma's cooking is more than just a feast for the senses; it's sensory overload.

I can just lay on my mat by the couch and watch Mom cook all day long. All the while, I am breathing in all the savory aroma she creates.

Sometimes, she goes outside to gather fresh herbs, and I follow her. And when she goes into the veggie garden, there are always peas or beans or berries ripe for picking; she even lets me pick a few too.

I always get a steak, pork, or lamb bone to gnaw on after dinner.

If there is any leftover sauce or drippings, Ma saves that and adds some broth to it. Then for a few days, I get that poured over my regular kibble ration in the morning and the evening.

I eat like a queen.

Since Ma is Italian, I think I am not a Labrador retriever but an Italian retriever.

Girls Only

Mom and I need a place where just us girls can go and not have any interruption or intrusion from Dad. We need our girl time so we can chat in private.

In front of the couch is our place; it's a girls-only area. Dad isn't welcome there.

If he ever enters our zone, I let him know he isn't allowed and nudge him away.

Mom sits on the couch and I lay at her feet next to the couch. We spend lots of special time there. We talk about everything; we even talk about Dad sometimes.

We really don't want Dad hearing what we say, especially what we say about him. LOL.

mischief

When Dad's not around or not paying attention, me and Mom can get into quite a bit of mischief.

For instance, when Mom's cooking it up in the kitchen, she often sneaks me extra special treats. Sometimes, she'll drop them into my feed bowl; when I hear them hit the bowl, I get up and come running over there to gobble them up.

I've become quite a taste-tester for Mom too. She lets me taste her recipes and asks me what she needs to add. I get a lot of goodies this way.

Other times, Mom will invite me to accompany her into the herb or veggie garden. This is always a chance for me to raid the strawberry patch or the blackberry vines. Sometimes, I even get away with nabbing a few beans and peas off the vine. Dad never even finds out.

This mischief is all in yummy good fun and really isn't all that bad; at least me and Mom don't think so. LOL.

Mamma's Pajamas

I take 'em and
   I shake 'em
   I bring 'em and
I fling 'em.
I sniff 'em and
I whiff 'em.
I snuggle with 'em, and
I cuddle with 'em.
I stare you, and
I dare you
to grab 'em and
to nab 'em.
My mamma's pajamas.

Retired

Dad has worked me hard all of my life, and I loved it. Over the years, I have walked thousands of miles and swam thousands of times. I was able to explore the natural world and meet many of the wild animals that live there.

Dad and I have kept a journal of our most memorable adventures.

But now Mom and Dad say I am retired. My hard-working days are over. I am pretty stiff and don't have the endurance I once had. Mom and Dad say I have earned a long and easygoing retirement life.

I must say I am sure enjoying it too. I get up when I want to. Mom brings me my bone and joint meds on a peanut butter scoobie; she brings them to me wherever I lie.

I eat whenever I am good and hungry, and that is pretty much anytime.

I still have short outdoor adventures with Dad, and I get to swim when the air and water are warm enough so that I don't get all stoved up.

I rest and relax a lot; I just enjoy spending time with Mom and Dad. After all, they are my best friends, and I really do love them.

I am enjoying my golden years, and I want to live forever.

Ol' Three Toes

Recently, I stubbed a toe and tore the nail on my front foot. It was very painful for weeks afterwards.

Mom and Dad took me to the vet, and I had my nail removed to the nub. I was given meds to take. I was okay for a short while, but the pain returned, and I could barely walk.

The vet thought my toe could be cancerous and said it was best to remove that toe and send it off to the lab for testing.

After the surgery, my foot was wrapped, and I was also on antibiotics and pain pills. My bandage had to be changed several times. Eventually, I had the bandage removed and my stitches pulled. Soon, I was pain free and walking again.

The lab results were positive, and the vet said the amputation would be curative.

All I can say is that I was so sick and tired of being sick and tired, and it felt so good to feel good again.

Mom and Dad say that I will be easy to track down because I am now known as Ol' Three Toes.

The Poop Police

Dad is the Poop Police. He has been checking my poop every day of my whole life. He says this is one way he monitors my health.

If I have worms or other parasites, he knows right away and treats me.

He can see if I have internal bleeding by looking at the color of my poop.

He can see what I have been eating, like grass or maybe foreign matter like plastic.

He wants to know if my poop is solid or runny, if it's soft or hard.

All this monitoring helps Dad head off any problems that might affect my health.

I have been healthy all my life; maybe it's because Dad has been policing my poop.

Alarm Clock

I have a biological clock in my head.

Mom needs to get up on time to go to work. Sometimes, she oversleeps or forgets to set her alarm clock. When this happens, I sense that she needs to get up, so I sound my alarm.

I come to her bedside and paw at her arm or flip it up with my snout to get her attention. Sometimes, I crash into the bed or stomp my back feet by the bed, making a lot of commotion to get her attention.

These things work too. Mom awakes and realizes that she needs to get up.

If you forget to set your alarm clock, don't worry. I will get you up.

Toy Box

I have a really great toy box at home. It's a nice wicker basket lined with a cloth mat that is solid red on one side and blue patterned on the other.

I keep my collection of balls in my toy box along with other toys like squeakers and my inchworm.

My favorite toy is my inchworm. Mom bought me my inchworm, and it's special. It was the very first toy she bought me. She mends it when the stuffing starts to come out of it; sometimes, I get pretty rough with it.

I can play pretty rough with my other toys too. Sometimes, I tear all the stuffing out of my squeaker toys, along with the squeaker itself. When I do this, Dad says I am gutting that toy. Mom and Dad have bought a lot of replacement squeaker toys for me.

All in all, my toy box is quite a treasure chest. Mom and Dad let me proudly display it in our living room.

Collection

Just like my dad, I have an awesome collection of my own.

Dad collects sea glass and sea shells when he goes beachcombing. I collect balls when I am on the trail or beachcombing with Mom and Dad. I have been collecting all my life.

Most of my collectables are old green tennis balls, but I also have quite a few special finds in my collection. I have a blue Air Dog squeaker ball, several different colored dog-paw print balls, and a brightly colored Chuck It ball.

When I find a ball I want to add to my collection, I carry it all the way back to the ol' black truck. When we get home, I bring the new ball into the house and it gets displayed in my toy box.

So far, I have collected about three dozen balls.

Romper Room

An old pup in her own romper room ... who ever heard of that?

Well, after last night's burst of playful antics, that is exactly what Mom and Dad say they have on their hands.

It all started after me and Dad had one of our usual rough-up sessions, where I crash into Dad and butt him with my head, and we just wrestle around with each other.

After this warm-up, I laid down and played catch with Dad with one of my tennis balls. He rolled the ball to me, and I threw it back to him either by batting it with my big ol' paw or by flinging it out of my mouth.

Then I got up and started spinning and whirling around until I grabbed up one of Dad's shirts off the floor. I shook that shirt from side to side like it was some animal I had hunted up and captured.

A few minutes of this, and I made a beeline for my toy box, where I snatched up and pounced on one of my squeaker balls.

That's when the real fun began. I poked at the ball with my snout until it squeaked back at me. Then I batted it with my paw and chased it down again and again, poking at it and trying to bring it to life.

Round and round our living room I chased that squeaking ball as Mom and Dad watched with delight and chuckled at my playful, puppy-like antics in my romper room.

I wore that poor ol' ball out, and after about twenty minutes, I had worn myself out too. So I went and crashed on the bed, and it was lights-out for me until next morning, just like any eleven-year-old pup.

Buster

One day, Buster arrived at the shelter. He was a Rottweiler/Mastiff mix breed of dog.

Buster was tall, dark, and handsome. He was very sweet, kind, and gentle. He had a regal quality about himself. I was smitten with Buster right away.

Once, he followed Dad right into our house. I was up on the couch. Normally, I might have become defensive if another dog came into our house, but Buster was a gentleman and very respectful.

He tred lightly into every room of our house and looked it over. He disturbed nothing.

Then, he came back into the living room and stood quietly by Dad. After that, he politely walked out of our house and waited for Dad to lead him back to his kennel.

Eventually, Buster was transported to the Humane Society in Portland and was soon adopted into a forever home.

Buster was a real prince of a dog; he was my prince.

Blinker

After a long cold night of violent thunderstorms, Dad took me outside early for my morning walk.

Right away, we saw a puppy tied to the main shelter gate out by the road. He was shivering and soaking wet. Dad put a leash on him and tried to lead him toward the kennels.

Immediately, we realized there was a problem. The pup was stumbling and very unsure of his footing. At closer look, Dad realized that he was blind.

Sure enough, the vet confirmed that Blinker, a six-month-old Catahula hound, was indeed totally blind.

Dad called Katie at Love Your Pet Sanctuary in northern California. This is a shelter that accepts special needs dogs. They had previously taken in Marley from our shelter. Marley was also a blind dog. Katie was also willing to take in Blinker, so Dad delivered him to her.

Blinker has had a great life at the sanctuary. He is happy, healthy, very friendly, and so smart.

Blinker has even helped train other blind puppies. Katie calls this program "the Blind Leading the Blind."

Dad says everyone can read about both Blinker and Marley at www.loveyourpetexpo.com. There you can see pics of Blinker. At this website, there is also a video of Blinker called "I Am a Happy Dog."

Goats

A small herd of eight mini-goats got impounded at the shelter. One day, they escaped their pen and began wandering all over the shelter grounds.

Dad and I set out to collect the goats and lead them back to their pen. We tried herding them; we tried leading them with a bucket of grain. Nothing worked; they remained very elusive and impossible to gather. We were at a stand-off and a stare-off.

Just then, Mom drove up to the main shelter gate out by the road. By now, the goats had wandered out that way and were dangerously close to escaping the shelter grounds and ending up on a very busy and dangerous road.

Mom saw our situation and climbed over the shelter gate. She picked a couple of bunches of tall grass and began sweet-talking the goats.

Just like the Pied Piper, she led those goats right back up the road toward their pen. It was like they trusted her and were saying, "We like you and will follow you wherever you lead us."

They marched right past me and Dad and left us standing in their dust, scratching our heads in bewilderment.

Mom had saved the day; she was a hero.

Later, when the goats were safely secured back in their pen, Mom just laughed and said, "You gotta know what their currency is."

Dolly

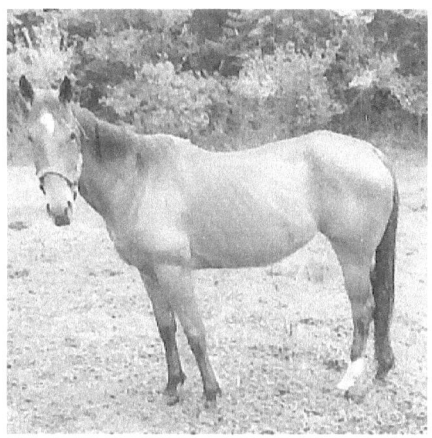

Well hello Dolly

Not only did Dad save the lives of dogs but he also saved a lot of horses.

Dolly was a six-year-old Quarter Horse mare who came to the shelter as a result of a law enforcement raid.

Dolly had been isolated in a small pasture with very little feed and water. She had very limited human contact for about two years. At 850 lbs., she was a rack of bones severely underweight and very weak. She was close to death.

It took a lot of time, tender loving care and patience for Dad and his staff to bring Dolly back to good health and high spirits.

With careful feeding, Dolly slowly began to add weight and strength to her frame.

A vet came to the shelter and wormed Dolly and vaccinated her for West Nile Virus and other equine diseases. Her teeth had to be floated, or filed down so that she could poperly chew her feed.

A ferrier came and trimmed her overgrown hooves and fitted her with horseshoes so that she could walk in comfort.

At six-years-old, Dolly was very head shy and not broke to saddle or ride.

After Dolly gained weight and strength, Dad's staff worked with her to make her more adoptable. Over time, Dolly was able to be haltered, saddled and rode.

I was curious about Dolly and sniffed at her through the corral fencing. Dad said that I should give her a lot of space so that she wasn't spooked or able to kick me. Dad said that she could hurt me if she kicked me.

After about eight months, Dolly weighed in at 1,250 lbs.. Her coat glistened and she was strong and healthy.

Dad took a special interest in Dolly. He loved Dolly and she loved him. Dad was the one who fed and watered her. He gave her special treats of carrots and apples throughout the day.

The horse corrals were next to Dad's office and Dolly would look through the window at Dad all day.

Dolly knew where we lived in Kennel #33. In the mornings when we awoke and turned lights on, Dolly would stand in the corral and stare at us from afar. At a certain time, she would begin to winnie, telling Dad she was ready for her morning feed.

At closing time, Dolly would winnie at Dad again, letting him know she was ready for her evening feed ration.

Dolly was thankful and grateful to Dad and his staff; she realized that they had saved her life.

There came a time when Dolly went up for adoption. Dad was very particular about who would adopt her. He wanted to make sure that she was never abused again and that she would have a good home.

A woman showed great interest in Dolly. Dad's staff inspected her property and its suitability for keeping a horse. They looked at her tack and evaluated her ability to afford keeping Dolly.

It was hard for Dad to let Dolly go. They had become very attached to each other.

It took the woman several months of visiting Dolly at the shelter to gain her trust and confidence. Dad and his staff tried to limit their daily contact with Dolly so that she could develop a new bond with the woman.

Eventually, Dolly was adopted and moved to her new home with lush green pastures along the Winchuck River. She settled into her life of regular trail riding and was very happy and content.

Dad says that Louis Armstrong said it best about Dolly in his song Hello Dolly--..*well hello Dolly! It's so nice to have you back.... you're looking swell.... I can tell Dolly....you're still glowin'...you're still goin' strong!*

The Cutter Cookie

Water has been my passion. I was born and bred to swim. Dad got me swimming when I was a baby, and I will never stop swimming.

I have swum in rivers, lakes, ponds, and even the ocean. I think about swimming all day long, and I even dream about it at night.

Dad says he loves to watch me spread my paws wide open and power effortlessly through the water.

He says the US Coast Guard should name a ship after me. If they did, he says they would christen it the US Coast Guard Cutter Cookie.

No way am I a cookie cutter dog; nope, I am the Cutter Cookie dog.

Bad Year

It's been a pretty bad year for me.

First of all, I had to get one of my front toes amputated; it was diseased and gave me a lot of pain. I could barely walk.

No sooner had I recovered from that surgery, than the fatty tumor on my hind quarters got so big I had to have that removed. It was so large that I had trouble sitting down and could not lay down on that side.

Mom and Dad took me in to the vet to get the fatty tumor removed. The vet said that it weighted about three pounds. After the surgery, I had more mobility and was able to lay down on either side again.

My arthritis still bothers me; the vet prescribed me some other meds just for my arthritis. Also I am still on my bone and joint supplements.

It's tough getting old.

We all look forward to a new and more pain-free year for me.

Warts

Like I said, it's tough getting old.

The mind is willing but the body isn't.

I'm stiff and sore and covered with growths everywhere: on my head, on my legs, and all around my neck.

It's tough getting old. The old gray mare just ain't what she used to be.

But Mom and Dad still love me, warts and all.

Momwich

Not only does Mom cook it up in the kitchen, but she also makes the best sandwiches on the planet.

She piles them high with awesome-tasting slices of meats like roast beef, chicken, and turkey.

She tops 'em off with delicious veggies like tomatoes, onions, sprouts, lettuce, olives, dill chips, arugula, and even cilantro.

Oh, I almost forgot to mention the cheese like cheddar, provolone, and even pepper jack.

All of this yummy goodness is held between slices of nutty bread or maybe a crispy roll.

Whenever we are out beachcombing or sea glass picking, none of us can wait for lunchtime.

Mom and Dad always make sure I get the last bite of each of their sandwiches (and most of the time, a few bites before the last one too).

What Mom makes isn't just a sandwich; no, it's a Momwich, made with lots of TLC.

Grilling Dog

Ahhh! This is summer at its best for canines: the sweet smoky smell of lamb, chicken, ribs, or T-bones on a sizzling hot grill.

And best of all, those tangy drippings drizzling down to the ground just for me to lap up. Mouthwatering and chop-licking good, fresh off the grill and cooked to perfection.

It doesn't get any better than this for a grilling dog like me.

Except maybe for those tasty bones I get to gnaw on after dinner.

Teeth

My vet says I have great teeth. He says they don't show my age at all.

I have never had bad breath, tooth decay, or even discoloration on my teeth.

I'm sure it's because of gnawing on knuckle bones, T-bones, and hard scoobie treats.

I have always been fed dry, hard kibble food twice a day.

Because of all of this, I still have my pearly whites.

Osprey

Fish eagles, also known as Osprey, have returned to our area. They are nesting along the river atop older and taller Douglas fir trees. They build big and sturdy nests.

When their young have hatched, they are busy fishing for food for themselves and their chicks.

As we walk along the river on our adventures, we often seem to present a danger to the osprey, and they will shriek loudly to warn us. Sometimes, they set off in flight and circle high above us, seemingly to size up the danger they think we pose them.

We keep moving along, and eventually the osprey settle down and go about their business of fishing and feeding their young.

Many times, we have seen them landing back at their nests with fish in their grip.

They are very impressive birds.

Opossum

Several times, an Opossum has wandered by our trailer at the animal control shelter.

If the dogs in the shelter detect the 'possum, they bark wildly at them. Then the 'possum starts hissing back at the dogs. Sometimes, this stirs the dogs up even more, and they jump up and rattle their kennel doors.

If the 'possum feels threatened by this, they do an amazing thing: They fall over, close their eyes and stick out their tongue, exposing their wicked-looking teeth. They are pretending to be dead.

They can lay like this for quite a while, until they sense the threat of danger has passed. Then they awaken and wander off to safety.

Dad says this is a real life demonstration of the phrase "playing 'possum."

It is quite a sight to see.

Brush Bunny

One of my favorite animal friends is the Brush Rabbit. I call them brush bunnies.

They are very beautiful and gentle creatures. They have nice reddish brown fur that really glistens in the sunlight. They have short ears and a small tail.

We see them cross the trail in front of us; sometimes they freeze in their tracks. We stand still and enjoy looking at them. They will stay motionless while standing in a patch of fresh and tender clover.

After we have admired them for a while, we begin to move forward. Then the bunnies will dart off into the brush for comfort and safety.

It's always a very special treat to see a brush bunny.

Sea Lion

Dad and I are always on alert for danger when we are on our adventures. We keep our eyes and ears peeled for any sign.

Just like mountain lions in the mountains, there are also lions in the sea: Sea Lions.

Our swimming hole is not far from where the river flows into the ocean. Because of this, there are times when sea lions are hunting for salmon running upriver to spawn. They swim right past our swimming hole while they are on the hunt. We can see their heads bobbing in the water; we can also hear them barking loudly.

Dad keeps me out of the water when sea lions are roaming the river. I am no match for such a big predator, especially one that can swim very fast.

Better safe than sorry.

Show Dog

It's a very special day for all of us when Mom comes along with me and Dad on our adventure.

I have my own way to celebrate these occasions. Mostly what I do is show Mom how big and tough I am.

I rip out bushes and shake them like captured prey. Dad will find the biggest and baddest sticks for me to retrieve out of the water.

Mom is always very impressed by how big, strong, and tough I am.

Dad says that he thinks I am a big show-off and calls me quite a show dog.

Security Dog

Mom and Dad don't need to install an expensive security and alarm system at home. I am all the protection they need.

When I see or hear something inside or outside, morning, noon, or night, that seems or appears to be threatening, I sound the alarm by barking.

If what I see or hear persists and becomes more immediate, I dial up the alarm by barking louder, snarling, and gnashing my teeth.

No intruder wants to be on the receiving end of my defense response because Labradors have some of the strongest jaws in the canine world.

The security of our home and the protection of Mom and Dad are my duty.

That's why I get the big scoobies.

Sweet Spot

Whenever I need to simmer down and unwind, Mom has the magic touch.

All she has to do is gently rub my lower belly, and all my stress and worry is relieved and relaxation sets in. I just lay on my back, close my eyes, and drift away to a blissful and carefree place. Sometimes, I can lay this way for an hour or more.

I can get to the same place when Dad rubs my sweet spot too. The only thing is I have to paw at Dad to get him to rub me in the right place. Mom has to tell him, "Cookie wants you to rub her sweet spot; she's trying to show you where she wants you to rub her."

Mom has the magic touch; Dad has to be shown most of the time.

Water Witch

When two-leggeds want to find water, they hire a geologist or a water witch to find it for them. They dig a well and tap into it.

When I'm on the trail, and it's hot and dry, I can nose out water; if it's there, I'm drawn to it.

Once I get scent of water, it's just a matter of time before I tap into it and lap it up. Cool, clean water is so refreshing. It tastes sweet and revives my strength.

Then to celebrate, I take a nice swim.

I love water.

Dad says I am a water witch.

Wasteland

Over the past six months, my stomping grounds down by the river have changed drastically

The property next to the river is owned by a construction and aggregate company. They have been hauling in tons of fill dirt and covering up nearly all the great habitat where we go for our adventures.

We are very concerned about what's going to become of our stomping grounds and all the wild animals that live there. We are seeing a lot fewer deer, wild turkeys, and other animals. Most of the teasels and cattails have been covered up.

We still have a narrow corridor next to the river that remains untouched and unaffected. We can still walk the trail along the river and pick blackberries.

We know that the rest of the area will all grow back, but that will take a long time.

It's sad for us to see our wonderland turned into a wasteland.

Luvrador

I love getting treats from my mom.

These are the treats that she gives me:

Every chance she gets, she wraps her arms around me and hugs me tight; she showers me with tons of kisses and tells me what a good dog I am; she says she is proud of me and that she loves me dearly.

Mom's treats are the best. They're even better than scoobies; they're sweet, and they fill my heart.

I'm just a big ol' Luvrador.

Reflections

Lucky Dog

My name was found in a fortune cookie, and indeed I am a very fortunate dog.

I depend on Mom and Dad for my care and protection. They meet my every need; I lack for nothing.

They have loved me every second of every day of my life.

I am a lucky dog.

The Good Life

I work hard, play hard, and sleep hard.

I'm active all day. From morning butt scratch stomp dances to daily walks and swims in the great outdoors to evening rough-ups, it's nonstop activity for me all day, every day.

Mom feeds me chop-licking good meals, and I'm provided a fresh pot of cool, clean water several times a day.

By the end of the day, I'm ready to hit the hay because:
Early to bed and early to rise
keeps a dog happy, healthy,
and energized.
It sure is a good life.
I'm living the canine dream.

The Best

For all he has done for me and for the life we have shared, I love my dad with all of my heart.

For all of her kindness, care, and protection of me, I love my mom with all of my heart.

They are the best mom and dad a dog could ever have.

True Blue

Dad tells me about a German shepherd dog from Argentina who has stood guard over his deceased owner's grave for six years.

When his owner passed away, the dog somehow found the cemetery and soon after that found his owner's grave site.

Until this day, the dog wanders the cemetery by day, until six o'clock, at which time he goes and lays atop his owner's grave, sleeping there until the next morning.

I have never left my dad's side whenever we are out for an adventure. I don't want to lose contact with him.

When Mom has to go to work, I anxiously await her return home, even watching out the window when I expect her to return home. I don't like us being apart.

Dad says this is the nature of the relationship between man and his dog; that they are inseparable; that they are true blue.

Me and Mom and Dad are a pack of three. We are true blue. Forever.

The Passing

Sunflower

Cookie was a bright and beautiful flower

Cookie lived a long, happy, and healthy life. She left us in a ray of sunshine.

On the day of her passing, she lay on a patch of cool, green clover and drew her last breath. Her mom was with her.

As she left us, doves flew in a flurry around our yard, and our metal wind chimes tinkled softly and so sweetly in a gentle breeze.

That very day, a big sunflower in our backyard burst into bloom.

Cookie was a rough-and-tumble girl, but she was also a very bright and beautiful flower.

Essence

This is the essence of Cookie:
    Her feet smell earthy, and
    her ears smell musty.
I love how the scent of her fills me up.
This is the essence of Cookie:
The deep, rich tone in her bark.
I love how beautifully that resonates.
This is the essence of Cookie:
The weight of her big ol' paw
as she slaps it down across my arm.
I love her dominance in play.
This is the essence of Cookie:
The clanging of the tags
on her old black collar.
I wear her tags around my neck now,
and when they clang,
it's Cookie I hear, and she is near.
And when I sniff her fragrant collar,
it's Cookie I smell, and she is with me.
We are together.

Universe

Like all dogs, Cookie remained dependent on her mom and dad her entire life. She counted on us for her care and protection. We were the center of her universe.

In return, she was loyal and protective of us, and she was our best friend. She was the center of our universe as well.

Then, Cookie got sick and had to go away. But that hasn't left a black hole. Our universe remains filled with her spirit, heart, and soul.

Kisses

Sometimes, riding in the ol' black truck, Cookie would suddenly sit up on the bench seat, look me straight in the eye, and give me a big ol' wet kiss on my face with her tongue.

And sometimes, Cookie would walk right over to Mom on the couch, look at her face to face, and give her a big ol' kiss too.

Cookie was very affectionate and freely gave us lots of kisses, letting us know how much she loved us.

She also loved getting kisses. She loved the kissy kissy sound we made with our lips when we kissed her on her head or her face and told her that we loved her.

Whenever Cookie was close by, love was in the air.

Dreams

Sound asleep at night, I often dream of Cookie.

While dreaming, I recall her when she was a tiny puppy, so innocent and filled with wonder.

I recall her thirst for learning. So curious and fearless, she ran freely and explored her world with reckless abandon.

I recall Cookie finding her passion for water, swimming, and retrieving.

I recall my realization that Cookie would always be dependent on me for her care and protection.

I recall that a Native chief once said, "Love a dog and derive great knowledge and power."

I recall my discovery that Cookie was teaching me as much as I was teaching her; that she was bringing routine and consistency to my life; that she was keeping my body fit and my mind sharp; that she was keeping me connected to the natural world; that she was bringing great adventure into my life; that she was keeping me company, proving her loyalty, becoming my best friend and partner.

I recall saying to myself, "Wow, all of this truly is great knowledge and power."

I recall how much Cookie loved her mom and how they shared the same heart.

I recall the day Cookie and I turned the exact same age; I recall how bittersweet that day was.

I recall Cookie growing older but remaining thirsty for adventure.

I recall her mom and I helping her climb up onto our bed and in and out of her ol' black truck.

I recall the smell of Cookie's ears and feet and what comfort that brought me.

I recall that Cookie, her mom, and I are a pack of three.

I recall my dog Cookie in my dreams at night, and I recall her when I am daydreaming too.

White Hawk

On the day that I drafted Laurie's dedication for this book, I just followed my pen as inspiration flowed freely across the paper. In no time, my dedication was written.

When I finished writing, I put my pen down, turned off the light in the man cave, and walked into the living room. As always, I looked out the sliding glass doors into our backyard.

There it was: a very light-colored Northern Harrier hawk. It was perched atop our backyard fence and peering directly at me; we were eye-to-eye. His big piercing eyes looked right into me. The white plumage of his head and chest was fluttering in the breeze.

No hawk had ever perched atop our fence before. Hawks had only soared across the sky, high above the treetops.

We looked into each other's eyes for a time. Then the white hawk turned itself around on the fence and gave me a view of his tailfeathers. In a few seconds, he lifted off and glided away into the distance.

This was Cookie at work. She sent this magnificent white hawk as a sign of her love and as a powerful expression of her approval for Mom's dedication.

What an awesome dog we have.

From the Milky Way

It's Me

That old black Lab with the gray muzzle and misty eyes who came to you at work and put her head in your hand the other day, that was me, Dad.

And two days later, that same old female Lab who put her paws up on your desk and looked into your eyes at your work, that was me, Mom.

And that brightly colored ball you found down by our swimming hole, the one just like in my toy box, I put that there for you, Dad.

I am up in the Milky Way, and
I am with you both.
Always and forever.
Love, Cookie

Dog Tags

My collar with my tags gave me my identity. Others knew who I was by reading my tags.

Who I was, was Mom and Dad's dog.

Now, I see that Dad wears my tags around his neck. He says he will wear them forever. Others know who Dad is by reading my tags.

Who he is, is Cookie's Dad.

Ashes

My ashes are contained in a cute dog-paw patterned metal container. Mom and Dad wrote loving words on my ash canister. They keep it close by them in their bedroom.

Mom talks to me and kisses my ash canister every morning.

One day, all of our ashes will be spread somewhere special, maybe at the beaver pond or along the river.

Memorial

One special way to remember loved ones is by memorial.

Dad has repurposed my feed trough into a living outdoor planter. The water side of my trough now has a pot inserted that is growing basil. Dad says this memorializes my love of Mom's cooking. She fed me like I was a queen. My meals were mouthwatering and chop-licking good.

The food side of my trough now has a pot inserted that is growing a blackberry plant. Dad says this memorializes my love of berry picking in the wild and in our garden.

Dad has repurposed my bulk dry food bin too. Now my bin is filled with Dad's socks. This celebrates my love of dragging out dirty socks (ducks) from the clothes hamper (the duck pond) and strewing them all over the house.

It sure is nice to be remembered.

Adventures

Dad still takes me on walks in the wild. Just like before, he brings my leash and safety whistle. He brings my scoobie jar with us as we ride along in my ol' black truck.

Dad still throws sticks into the water for me to retrieve.

I still pick blackberries along the river, and Dad still picks the best-tasting and juiciest ones for me, and he still feeds them to me out of his hand.

I loved my adventures before, and I love them now too.

Dad let me run free before, and he lets me run free now too.

Everything is still the same as it was before, and it always will be.

Sharing

I am sharing my amazing life with all the other dogs up here on the dog way. They love hearing all about my adventures and about my mom and dad.

It is bittersweet, though, because some of the dogs weren't as fortunate as me and had heart-breaking lives before.

I need to talk to Dad about doing something about that situation down there.

The Promise

Dad, I want you to know that you kept the promise you made to me so long ago as we rode along in the ol' black truck on our way home.

Not only did you fulfill your promise but you filled my life with so much more.

You were the greatest guardian a dog could have. You kept me safe; you gave me freedom; you showed me the world; and you taught me so much. You were a devoted and loyal friend.

You were all of this and more to me then.
You are all of this and more to me now.
You are my dad, and
I am your dog now, always, and forever.
This, I promise to you, Dad!
Love, Cookie

Afterword

The Calling

For six years, Cookie watched thousands of dogs and other animals enter the shelter that I managed.

Too many of these animals came in scared, infested, infected, injured, starved, dehydrated, blinded by light, unable to stand or walk, stained with feces and urine, beaten, tortured, and otherwise neglected or abused.

I saw Cookie's concern; she sensed their pain.

Now, she's up in the Milky Way where the spirits and souls of animals arrive after they pass from this earth. Too many arrive with wounded souls and lonely hearts, so thirsty for restoration.

How tragic for such innocent creatures, and especially for dogs, sent to us as gifts from God, whose only desire is to find their best friend, the one who will love and care for them.

I hear Cookie calling.

She is calling to me, "Do something, Dad. Please help end the suffering down there."

I hear her calling.

The Answer

Gandhi said the greatness of a nation can be judged by the way its animals are treated.

Based on this standard, we have a lot of hard work ahead of us before we truly achieve greatness as a nation.

No one of us can save every animal in need, but we all can make a difference.

Hear the call. Answer the plea.

If you suspect neglect or abuse, notify your local animal control or law enforcement agency.

Volunteer to walk dogs at your local animal shelter. Offer to transport dogs to rescue organizations. Donate needed supplies to your local shelter. Offer to foster a dog at your home. Make a monetary donation to the Humane Society or the ASPCA.

Hear the call. Answer the plea.

Make a difference and help save the lives of Man's Best Friend.

Appendix 1

RESPONSIBLE PET OWNERSHIP

Rabies and other vaccinations kept current

Exercise and explore the outdoors with your dog

Select a breed that fits your lifestyle

Patience, attention and interaction with your dog

Obedience training

Nutrition and clean drinking water

Spay/Neuter your dog at a young age

ID, license and rabies tags on collar

Brush and inspect for pests regularly

Leash and collar your dog

Enjoy your dogs- they're family

Appendix 2

Building A ProLife Shelter

The Foundation-

Agreements with non-profit rescue organizations and animal sanctuaries to transfer dogs to facilities with more opportunities for adoption.

Certified volunteer program to augment and support local shelter resources.

Administrative policy for owner surrender of dogs to control and limit the intake of adoptable animals.

The Keystone-

Official county administrative policy on euthanasia.

* The California state policy on euthanasia of adoptable and treatable animals is found in California Penal Code Section 599d and California Food and Agriculture Code Section 17005. These sections were adopted, by reference, locally to set in place the keystone for a ProLife animal control shelter in Del Norte County, California.

Search for similar sections of law in your state.

About the Author

Ken Smith has spent a lifetime exploring the natural world. Activities like boating, fishing, hiking, camping, skiing, and photography have filled him with a deep reverence and respect for the natural world.

It's no wonder then that his beloved dog Cookie and he were a perfect fit for outdoor adventures.

Ken enjoyed a rewarding thirty-eight-year career as a public servant. The last six years of his career were spent as Director of Animal Control at a small shelter in northern California.

There he inherited a high-kill, borderline humane shelter operation. Nearly half of the dogs who entered the shelter were euthanized.

Working closely with the local Humane Society and with the support of the county Board of Supervisors, he transformed his shelter into an ultra-low-kill pro-life animal control facility.

During his last five years as Director of Animal Control, Ken maintained a kill rate of just 1 percent. He was instrumental in moving the Board of Supervisors to adopt a policy that stopped the destruction of any adoptable or treatable dog.

Private owner surrender of dogs to the shelter was greatly reduced; instead, dog owners were given a networking guide so that they could find suitable homes for their unwanted dogs.

Ken placed a bed in every kennel and got dogs up off the cold concrete floor.

Money was approved in his budget for first aid and emergency vet care for shelter dogs.

Dogs entering the shelter began to be vaccinated by staff for protection against a wide range of canine diseases.

A standard and consistent diet began to be fed to dogs at the shelter.

Dogs infected with contagious diseases were being isolated, treated, and cured at a high rate of success.

With assistance from the local Humane Society, an army of public volunteers was trained and certified to walk dogs and provide other support to shelter staff.

The Board of Supervisors approved a memorandum of understanding between the county and legal nonprofit rescue organizations. This allowed the transfer of shelter dogs to other adoption facilities and rehab sanctuaries. All transfer fees to these organizations were waived.

An extensive networking system was put in place. Soon, a catalog of rescue organizations and benefactors was compiled. Dogs were being transferred all across the western United States, and monetary donations for individual dogs in need were being received from as far away as New York City.

Shelter dogs soon overcame depression and had a spring in their step. In spite of their circumstances, most of the dogs were happy.

Employees at the shelter soon started looking forward to coming to work instead of dreading it.

Saving the lives of dogs and other animals was becoming infectious and exciting.

Literally thousands of canine lives were being saved.

Ken's shelter had left the dark ages of animal control and emerged into the light of a new era. The pro-life approach to animal control was born.

His time as Director of Animal Control became the most rewarding of his entire career.

Now retired, Ken lives with Laurie, his wife and Cookie's mom, in southern Oregon.

Together, they often recall the amazing life of adventure they shared with their beloved dog Cookie and those challenging but rewarding days spent saving the lives of Man's Best Friend.

www.ingramcontent.com/pod-product-compliance
Lightning Source LLC
Chambersburg PA
CBHW030321100526
44592CB00010B/515